DUNCAN CAMPBELL —
A BIOGRAPHY

DUNCAN CAMPBELL —
A BIOGRAPHY

The Sound of Battle

by

Andrew Woolsey

HODDER AND STOUGHTON
LONDON SYDNEY AUCKLAND TORONTO
and
THE FAITH MISSION

Dedicated to

Mrs. Shona Campbell

Contents

Preface

A CASUAL reader of the Acts of the Apostles could easily assume that the lives of the early apostles were above mundane duties, seeing only drama upon drama, miracle following miracle in rapid succession, continual scenes of revival and glory, until with a final, fiery leap those heroes of faith welcomed their eternal embrace.

It is easy to miss the little conjunctive verses which link the outstanding events of their lives, and tell us that in certain places they 'abode long time' or 'continued there a year and six months'. Doing what? Nothing spectacular! Patiently dealing with vexing problems of church, home and personal life; just demonstrating the life of Jesus in the humdrum setting of every-day circumstances.

Biographies similarly tend to concertina the outstanding events of life for quick observation, giving the impression of lives with which we could never be identified, men and women whose faith we could never follow, but it is not so. Between the stirring incidents are periods of silence that speak for themselves, with nothing to record but the multitude of petty burdens that weigh heavily on human spirits from day to day.

9

Duncan Campbell was no stranger to these. He was familiar with times of barrenness and depression; the burdens and cares of family life, and ordinary duties occupied much of his time. But he learned a secret: that to practise the presence of God and live for Jesus in that setting is as glorifying to God as the emotional upheaval in scenes of revival.

For various reasons human biographers seldom tell the whole story; there are trials and testings, faults and failings which remain undisclosed, and the subject of the following story is no exception. While he was above many in spiritual stature, he also had his failings—sometimes sore and shattering. But out of the ashes of deep repentance rose a chastened, humbled spirit and a more Christlike life to take God's message to others.

It was a rare privilege to know him. He was a very ordinary man, but he was different. People meeting him were introduced to new spiritual dimensions, and could never be the same again. It is this difference that makes the story of his life worth telling.

It is usually after a considerable lapse of time that the fullest picture of a life can be seen. The farther we move from the base of the mountain the clearer we view the whole and are better positioned to appreciate its salient features. Likewise, we are as yet too close to the lifetime of Duncan Campbell to evaluate clearly the full strength and influence of his life and ministry.

This biography is not the work of an individual but of a small army of friends and acquaintances too numerous to mention, each one making a distinctive contribution, and to all of whom I am deeply indebted. The story is written with the earnest prayer that God will bless the effort to extend posthumously Duncan Campbell's much needed ministry, and bring to a new generation of

Christians the reality of what God can do in and through a life that is placed utterly at His disposal.

What God has done for one, He can do for others. May the following pages inflame our desire for God and quicken our steps until the sound of battle is heard more loudly in the lives of the Redeemed bringing revival in its wake.

A. A. W.
Edinburgh
November 1973

CHAPTER ONE

Fighting Forebears

THE 13th of February is a date that no Campbell cares to remember. The briefest account of Highland history recalls the shameful deed which makes the Clan suspect to this day in at least one Scottish glen. It even seems to be recorded in the very landscape of the magnificent, melancholy valley of Glencoe—the Glen of Weeping.

An oath of allegiance was required by the Government before 1st January, 1692. The head of a small community of MacDonalds in Glencoe delayed appearing at the Sheriff's Court, and because of adverse weather conditions failed to arrive in time.

A detachment of soldiers under Captain John Campbell of Glen Lyon was dispatched to the village. It was well known that the Campbells and MacDonalds had many old scores to settle. The soldiers were kindly received for two weeks, but on orders from Ballachulish they betrayed Highland hospitality and during the night put their hosts to the sword. Some, warned by the soldiers, escaped, but on that dark and bloody morning, thirty-eight people died in cold blood and others perished in the cold as they fled.

Two-hundred-and-six years later, to the day, the

baby-cry of another fighting Campbell was heard in a plain, three-roomed house in North Connell. This child was destined to carry not a sword of destruction to these northern regions, but the Sword of the Spirit which is the Word of God. Through his voice the message of salvation would one day penetrate thousands of Highland hearts, including many MacDonalds.

His family history boasts a few famous names of poets, statesmen and soldiers, including Sir Colin Campbell, Commander-in-Chief of the Highland Brigade in the Crimean War and the Indian Mutiny, but the ancestral records are also humble enough to record that not all the battles of his fighting forebears were as honourable as Balaclava or the Relief of Lucknow!

A paternal ancestor, Campbell of Ardkinglas, owned a large estate in the heart of Campbell country near to Inveraray, with its magnificent castle, the home of the Dukes of Argyll.

In those days the system of patronage was practised in Scotland. The kirk was supported by the State. Plausible enough, but the crunch came when the State called the tune and decided what the church should teach and how it was to be governed. Also under this system the 'parish minister' was elected by the State, mainly on the recommendation of the local laird or some other aristocrat in the community. These gentlemen in spite of their wealth and influence, or perhaps because of it, were not always favourable to the gospel of Christ or anxious to fashion their lives according to its teaching. Consequently it became desirable because of social and material advantages to have a younger son, or an eligible male relative in the church, regardless of character or spiritual experience.

The ancestor from Ardkinglas must have been well known for he had two brothers in the ministry! The sad fact is that neither he nor his brothers were qualified to have the honour of the kirk in their custody. One day these two met in an hotel in the seaside town of Oban and, as the manner is when too much liquor has been consumed, a dispute arose.

'If it wasn't for the collar, I'd hammer you,' one shouted.

'Take the collar off then,' was the quick retort.

It was duly done, and the two 'reverend' gentlemen stepped out into Argyll Square, and amid scenes reminiscent of the Wild West, fought like tigers until the quarrel was settled. It is not known what scars graced the occupants of the pulpit on the following Sabbath!

The estate of Ardkinglas was eventually lost through dissipation, and Duncan's grandfather secured a farm in 'the wild region of Benderloch' at the head of the Firth of Lorne, on the rugged Argyllshire coastline. All went well until he became surety for a friend with business interests in America. The firm went bankrupt and he lost everything. But he fought back, and after years of struggle managed to survive, perhaps more due to grandmother's thriftiness than his own!

The Campbells are a proud clan, even in poverty. Grandfather Campbell exemplified this. He always sported a kilt and other items of national dress, but one day when he overspent to add a further piece of finery to his regalia, grandmother, in her effort to keep bread on the table, had something to say!

Nevertheless, he was a clever man with an excellent grasp of the English language and in a community where only Gaelic was spoken he was asked to interpret for English tourists. Another task he performed was to administer an old cure for certain diseases by putting leeches on to the veins of his patients to suck the blood.

The knife he used for this crude work is still serviceable, but one look at it would be enough to make a modern surgeon shudder!

Hugh Campbell came next in the line of ancestry. He took up a good solid occupation as a stone mason to help the family budget, and when his fancy took flight he looked around with typical Scottish prudence to seek a lassie that would make him a 'guid wife'. His working interests at that time extended to a small farm which his father had bought on the shores of Achnacree Bay, at the mouth of Loch Etive, a long narrow sea loch, steeped in beauty, history and romance, that winds its way through the hills, with its headwaters in Glen Etive.

The eyes of the young seeker blinked with approval when they rested on Jane Livingstone with her deep brown eyes, high brow, full lips and wavy, brunette hair, swept into a bun at the back.

Jane Livingstone was born on the nearby island of Lismore, a long, green finger of land across the Lynn of Lorne, famed in poetry and picture for its horizon that thrusts the glory of the evening sunset across the sky in a blaze of bewitching colours.

Her immediate family background is rather obscure, but the trail in search of ancestral lore yields at least one interesting item. The Livingstones who lived on Lismore were of the same family as another of that name, who hailed from the small basaltic island of Ulva, off the west coast of Mull. A branch of this family moved to Blantyre in Lanarkshire. There, in humble circumstances, a boy, David Livingstone, was born whose dust now lies with that of kings and statesmen in Westminster Abbey, and whose life was spent as a missionary explorer in Central Africa, fighting to bring the light of the gospel and the liberties of civilisation to the people of the 'dark continent'.

However distant this link with the famous explorer may be, Hugh Campbell's bride carried the same native dignity and patience in Achnacree that David Livingstone displayed in Africa. She became the mother of ten children, all with sturdy family names. It was no small task to rear a large family at a time when the child mortality rate was high and money was scarce, but with an indomitable spirit and modest joy Jane Campbell devoted her life to her calling and dreamed her dreams for their future.

CHAPTER TWO

Camus-liath

THE district where Hugh Campbell and his young
bride set up home was known as Blackcrofts; the former
part of the title having no reference to paint or pitch, but
to the character of those who first lived there. Years
before, when it was desolate, unclaimed country, the
landlord at Loch Nell Castle decided to use it as a
natural penitentiary for sheep-stealers and tax-defaulters.
Each one was given a spade to till the land, and tools to
build a house, and banished to this wilderness to fend for
himself. As a result, ten crofts sprang up on the foreshore.
Blackcrofts was there to stay.

The Campbell croft, *Camus-liath*—the grey estuary—,
was situated a little farther along the shore from these.
The Campbell children during their school-days used to
boast that their home was not one of the original '*black
crofts*' with its stigma from the past hanging over them.

It was here that Highland air first filled the lungs of
Duncan Campbell.

The Rev. J. A. MacCormack sprinkled water on the
child's forehead according to the traditional mode of
baptism and, with his name duly entered in the records of
the Kirk Session in Ardchattan Parish Church, the boy

17

took his place in the home and community with the prayers of the faithful surrounding him, and with the rather dubious promise that he would be brought up in the fear, and nurture, and admonition of the Lord; for at that time his parents, like Samuel of old, 'did not yet know the Lord'.

But in 1901, when Duncan was still a toddler, just graduated from the creeping stage, something happened that changed the course of life in the Campbell home. Two girls came to Benderloch.

Fifteen years before, a young Glasgow businessman, John George Govan, received a commission to evangelise in the country districts of Scotland and Ireland. His home became a Bible-training centre where young people came to study the Bible and learned to know God in a personal, practical way. Like the early disciples of Jesus they went out in twos without any guaranteed support, but with faith in God to supply their needs, and to use His Word through them to save men and women.

Wherever they could secure premises, whether a church, hall, school or barn, these young men and women prayed, preached and sang the good news of salvation.

Women preachers are still frowned upon in the Highlands of Scotland but in those days they were unheard of. It caused no small stir when Maggie Campbell and her co-worker arrived in Ledaig to preach.

Who did they think they were? Well, the people came out to see. They called themselves 'Pilgrims', and wore straw bonnets with a fringe of velvet round the front issuing in ribbons that reached below the chin and came together in a neat little bow.

But when the novelty of their appearance wore off and the folk began to listen to what they had to say, it was no new thing. Was this not what John Campbell, the Bard of Benderloch, had preached for forty years in his cave at Ledaig?

This talented gentleman had transformed a natural cave among the rocks into a place of worship. Seats were placed in the curve of the rock, and from a small table, said to have been made from a tree against which Robert the Bruce leaned on returning from a fight with MacDougall of Lorne, this doughty evangelist taught the good news of 'another king, one Jesus', to crowds of young people who gathered in what must have been one of the most unique preaching places in Scotland.

The Pilgrims were also of Highland stock. Maggie Campbell had pioneered the work of the Faith Mission for eleven years throughout the Western Highlands and Islands, enduring much hardship to win souls for Christ. She loved people, and from her little platform, with tears streaming down her face, pleaded with them to come to Christ. On one occasion when a convict ship was about to sail to the outer islands she persuaded the captain to allow her to accompany them to speak about the Saviour. Now, following the footsteps of the famous bard, she sought to win the hearts of the people of Benderloch for her Master.

Amid the pressures of family life Hugh Campbell and his wife found time to attend the Pilgrims' meetings and the great turning point was reached. With their eldest boy they both gave their allegiance to Jesus Christ and started to follow Him. It is impossible to assess the far-reaching influence of this major miracle in the life of any human being, and more so if that one is a parent. Like ripples from a stone cast into water it reaches out to succeeding generations.

Family worship became part of life at *Camus-liath*.

'The hallowed power and sacred influence of this devotional exercise' has left a deep impression on Scottish life. The scene is depicted by Burns in *The Cottar's Saturday Night:* The head of the home 'tak's the buik', a Psalm is sung, followed by a reading from the Bible, and then prayer is offered for the family and for the work of God.

This Hugh Campbell did each Sabbath morning, before taking his place in the Precentor's pulpit in the local church to lead the congregation in singing the Psalms of David.

During the week he left home each morning at five-thirty. It fell then to his devoted wife to conduct the daily devotions. It was no burden to her. Prayer was as vital as breathing. She prayed with the children, and when alone prayed for them. Each morning as they were leaving for school, she sat down by the fireside and, reverently tossing an apron over her head, kept a sacred tryst with her Saviour.

With the cries of four other 'bairns' already heard in the home, and five more still to follow, there was little time for the fifth child of Hugh Campbell to be spoiled. From the time he was knee-high in the heather on Ben Lora, overlooking the home, he was expected to pull his weight with the chores around the croft. In the kitchen was a big open fireplace with its crook and chain. A pair of hand-bellows stood in the corner and on one side was an old-fashioned oven where Jane Campbell baked for the family. On the other side a griddle was often laden with oatcakes or bannocks.

That fire needed fuel, and fuel in those days was peat cut from the bog that stretched across the moor between Blackcrofts and the village of Benderloch. Every summer the children, barefooted, helped to cut, carry, and stack the peats. It was hard work but they enjoyed it and looked forward to it, though many an evening under the flickering oil-lamp it was a 'wearie laddie' who turned down the big wooden seat in the kitchen, and tumbled into the box-bed that supplemented the sleeping quarters. Then before the three-mile walk to school each day peats had to be taken in for Mother and the big churn outside the door filled with water from the well, and 'don't forget to brush out the byre before you go!' The three cows housed up there, turning out daily nourishment for hungry youngsters, needed attention.

Potatoes, kale and corn were grown on the land. In the evenings, the latter was threshed with flails, as it was needed. The larder was also replenished from the sea. On a summer evening when Hugh Campbell returned from his stone building he would call: 'Get the tackle, Duncan. We'll take the small boat tonight.' No second invitation was needed. Duncan was perfectly at home sailing a boat. Mackerel, lythe, sea trout and cuddies were brought ashore, and after the first meal the remainder were salted for later use.

Indoors, Jane Campbell found time in the evenings to spin yarn which was woven into cloth to provide suits for the family. Days were full at *Camus-liath*, but even with an increasing family and increased activity, God was worshipped and honoured.

The greater influence for God in the lives of the Campbell children was undoubtedly on the maternal side. Jane Campbell, from the moment of her conversion, walked consistently with the Saviour and lived a beautiful Christlike life. In her the children found a friend in whom they could confide.

She was seldom seen on the road, except on the way to church. The home was her kingdom. All problems were referred to her, and found satisfying answers. Her knowledge of the Scriptures was uncanny, and masculine pride took a beating when questions of a theological nature were taken to Mother. She had a wonderful gift for unravelling the mysteries of grace. But while never away from home, the magnetism of her personality attracted others to her. 'We loved to go there,' remarked one who frequently found his way to her home and no doubt to her prayers. Thus she lived, and loved, and prayed until in old age, after much suffering, with the Bible still propped up before her and a heavenly light glowing on her face, she fell asleep in Jesus.

Duncan never forgot the debt he owed to his mother. How thankful he was that he had a mother who knew God. With tender care and many an anxious prayer she watched over the determined wee fellow with the shock of bright red hair as he worked and played around the croft.

His brother describes him as a 'wee rascal' and very independent. He always put into practice what he believed and would risk the wrath of anyone to defend his pals. Willie MacDougall was a favourite. They were inseparable. He was the same age as Duncan and lived in the croft on the hill. But Willie was full of mischief which sometimes brought trouble on himself and his friends. One day the school-teacher, a minister's daughter, and a well-built girl, was attempting to moderate Willie's mischievous sport with a belt. After a few switches Duncan could stand it no longer. He jumped up and caught her by the skirt to rescue his pal, but in the midst of the drama her waist-band suddenly snapped. For a sedate Highland schoolmistress to have to hold her skirt up with one hand and administer corporal punishment with the other was no light task, but she laughed heartily as later she told the story to his elder brother!

His schoolfriends describe him as adventurous and courageous. When the teacher walloped Jamie MacIntyre on the bare legs he hopped, but wallop Duncan and he showed no sign of pain. He was quick to accept a challenge. When dared to jump the wide drains along the bog road on the way from school, he did not always arrive home dry. Another day his bravado came to grief when he climbed into a large hawthorn-tree, forgetting that thorns are sharp until one pierced his hand. He let go and the result was a broken leg and a ride home in Neil Black's cart, suffering more from wounded pride than a wounded leg.

On leaving school his first job was to work as a 'herd' for the local crofters. The cows, kept in all winter, were taken out daily during the summer months to the communal grazing that bordered the peat-bog near to Lochan-an-ra. Early in the morning he collected his charges, and with a 'piece' for lunch set off to ensure that none wandered into the bog.

On sunny days he would sit on the stone cairn by the loch; if it rained he would shelter in a little house he had built with stones from the shore and roofed with heather and whin bushes. A visitor to the district took an interest in the 'wee herd laddie', and when he saw this construction wrote a poem in broad Scots entitled *The Herd's Hoose*, which years later was recited on the radio and also appeared in one of Scotland's leading newspapers.

The wee herd laddie has biggit a hoose,
   He's biggit it a' his lane;
And there he can lie, and watch his kye,
   And fear nae wind nor rain.

He has pickit the place w' a skilly thocht,
  On a knowe at the end o' the bight;
And the door looks east where the wind blows last,
  And his charges are a' in sicht.

It's twa foot wa's are o' tide marked stanes,
  That the waves hae masoned round;
And ilka bit chink, where the day micht blink,
  Wi' fog he has oakumed sound.

It's roofed and thickit, a tradesman's job,
  The rafters are runts o' whins;
Wi' bracken and heather, weel soddit thegether,
  And wechtin' stanes abune.

There's an ingle nook, at the hinmaist en',
  And the lum was a pail in its day;
And out at the back, there's a wee peat stack
  As any bit hoose should hae.

He'll fen' for himsel' a laddie like yon,
  And lang may he live to tell,
When he's feathered his nest, and come
  home for a rest,
O' the wee hoose he biggit himsel'.

What thoughts passed through Duncan's mind as he
sat alone with his cows we do not know. He had a lot
to think about; his mother's teaching and example; the
long talks with his eldest brother, Donald, who had been
blinded by a flying staple when erecting a fence on his
uncle's farm in Mull, but whose inner sight was opened
to the Light of the world; and the instruction of his
Sunday School teachers at Alt-na-mara, in the hall

built to commemorate the work of John Campbell, not far from the cave where he preached. We do know that from childhood he thought deeply and out on the moor, with the sun tanning his features and the wind beating, impressions were deepened to an awareness of God in nature that were to crystallise into a personal knowledge of God through the miracle of re-birth.

Meantime other attractions were on the horizon. The local concerts appealed strongly to the young folk. At these, sketches were enacted and demonstrations given at piping and sword-dancing, followed by the traditional square-dancing accompanied by an accordion. Performers were popular, and having become acquainted with a wider circle of friends on commencing his apprenticeship in a grocer's shop in Connell Ferry, the one-time 'herd laddie' thought it would be better to become a proper 'Heilan' laddie.' He acquired a chanter, and practised step-dancing. A cousin of his father, who was an expert piper, gave him lessons. He was now stepping up in the world. With a good job, living a respectable life and enjoying local popularity what more could he need?

CHAPTER THREE

Over the Top

A CONCERT was in full swing. On the platform stood a young piper, known locally as *Am Piobaire Ruadh*—the Red Piper. Belts and buckles shone in the dim light. Kilt and sporran, Glengarry bonnet and ribbons completed his colourful regalia.

It was December 1913. Across Europe war-clouds were threatening. It seemed a far cry from Benderloch, but the Argyll Nursing Association was anxious to boost its funds, so a concert and dance was arranged.

During an interlude the piper was playing by request a well-known Scottish tune, *The Green Hills of Tyrol*, which he had played recently at the local Games. It is a plaintive air that fills Scottish hearts the world over with overwhelming nostalgia and the skirl of the instrument, pouring out its eulogy of the 'hills of home', was captivating the young Highland audience as only pipe music can do.

But as he reached the second part of the tune a remarkable thing happened. Confidence went out of his performance. His thoughts were suddenly transported to another green hill, not in Austria or Scotland, but outside the wall of Jerusalem in Palestine. He could hear the dull blow of a hammer echoing faintly among the rocks and see spectators milling around or huddled in little groups. Some talked excitedly, some laughed and jeered, others gasped in horror or wept silently. A man was being nailed to a cross and raised with two others in view of the crowd. Every eye was on the central figure. Why was *He* there? He had done no wrong.

Suddenly the young piper felt in some way responsible for His death. Terrible conviction of sin seized him, and a sense of desolation and lostness swept over him. As he focused his attention again on present surroundings the question kept coming: 'Is this all that life has to offer a young fellow?'

With difficulty he finished the section he was playing, and turning to the other pipers beside him said: 'Boys, you carry on, I'm going home.' The chairman of the concert, who had invited him to play and also to demonstrate his skill at step-dancing, was sitting nearby. Duncan approached him: 'I'm sorry, I'll have to go.'

'Go, where?'

'I'm going home, and unless I'm greatly mistaken I'll never be at a dance again.'

'Why? What's wrong? Are you ill?'

'There's nothing wrong with my body; I'm disturbed in my mind. It's my sin. I'm troubled about my sin.'

'Oh,' smiled the sceptical chairman, 'You'll soon get over that.'

But the impressions on his mind were too deep to shrug off easily. Amid the chatter and laughter of his companions he had come within the drawing power of the cross of Jesus Christ and was caught in the grip of God. The irresistible power of the Holy Spirit was now operating within him. God had a tryst with his soul before the morning light would break—a tryst that must

be kept. So with the questioning looks of the young folk
he had been entertaining following him, Duncan picked
up his instruments and left the hall.

Robert Browning wrote that it is

> ... when the fight begins within himself,
> A man's worth something. God stoops o'er
>   his head,
> Satan looks up between his feet—both tug—
> He's left, himself, in the middle: the
>   soul wakes ...

When a man hears the voice of God he realises that
life is a more serious business than he imagined before.
Aware that he is no longer an autonomous creature in his
own little world, accountable to no one, he feels eternity
within, and with horror sees himself without an anchor
on the sea of life, cut off from God because of what he is
and what he has done. The powers of the unseen world
are real and his soul becomes a battleground. Within
rages the fight for right against wrong. God's way or his
own way? He must decide. And the battle within will be
won or lost on the ridge of repentance. To turn from his
own way and go over the top, dying to the past, and
casting all upon the mercy of God will take him forward
into a new life of victory in Christ. But should he baulk at
that ridge and therefore fall back, he may, like King
Herod, silence forever the voice of God to his soul.

A battle was lost and another won on the lonely
Benderloch road that December night. Another young
man fell into step with Duncan as he started for home.
He, too, was troubled by an inner conflict. Perhaps he
had been at the dance and overheard the conversation
with the chairman. We don't know. But as the two lads

walked they discussed their state and the way of salvation so familiar to them. Reaching a road junction they
stood for a long while before parting.

'What are we going to do?' his companion asked
eventually.

'Well, I don't know about you,' said Duncan, with a
note of finality, 'but I'm going home to get right with God
tonight.'

'I think I'll wait a while,' the other responded hesitantly.

He waited until he grew into manhood, became a
successful businessman, and eventually in old age was
taken into a nursing home to die. Questioned about his
spiritual state and urged to seek Christ he sullenly
replied: 'Speak no more to me on that matter. I settled it
the night Duncan was saved.'

The conflict had ceased, and even by the door of
death he had no desire for mercy. Duncan later wrote of
a similar tragedy: 'In the crisis of life, the supreme
moment of his history, he failed. He sacrificed principle
for a little earthly gain, forgetting that in the bargain he
bartered his own soul.'

One battle was lost.

Duncan with a heavy heart continued the three-mile
walk along the road he had so often skipped as a boy
without a care in the world. Now it seemed as if the whole
world and the very heavens were crushing in upon him.

Turning a corner at Alt-na-mara, he suddenly halted.
There was a light in the small Memorial Hall where he
had attended Sunday School. He couldn't understand it.
A light in the church at eleven o'clock! What did it mean?
Being away from home, helping Angus MacSwan to open
a new shop in Corpach, near Fort William, he was
unaware of the 'goings on' in the district and had only
returned that evening for the dance.

Drawn to the building with more than mere curiosity
he could hear someone praying and, putting his ear to the
keyhole, recognised the voice of his own father.

Gently he turned the handle and entered. Leaving the
bagpipes and two swords, which he used for dancing, on
the back seat, he tiptoed up the aisle and sat down. When
he had finished praying Hugh Campbell turned in
amazement to see at his side the son for whom he had
been praying and simply said: 'I'm glad to see you here,
Duncan. Mother was praying for you last night.'

On the platform the United Free Church minister sat
between two strange girls dressed in peculiar bonnets.
The Pilgrims, of course! He hadn't seen them for years
and had almost forgotten what they looked like. Mary
Graham from Skye and Jessie Mowat, a girl from
Aberdeen, were conducting a mission and with a few
local Christians were now engaged in a night of prayer.

Others prayed and then Mary rose to her feet, quoted a
verse from the Bible, and started to preach. The text was:
'God speaketh once, yea twice, yet man perceiveth it not'
(Job 33:14).

The conscience of the newcomer was so stung by her
words that he had to hold on to the seat to stop trembling.
Eventually, fearing he would create a scene by remaining
longer, he rose quickly, picked up his instruments on the
way out, and proceeded home.

On the way, he dropped to his knees again and again
by the roadside, crying to God for mercy. It was late,
around 2 a.m., when he turned down the path to *Camus-
liath*.

For the second time that night he was amazed to
discover a light burning at a late hour. His mother was
still on her knees by the kitchen fire. Relatives had
arrived and she was unable to attend the prayer-meeting

with her husband, but when they had gone to bed she joined in spirit with those in the hall to pray for God's blessing upon the mission and for her own family.

Duncan sat down beside her, and like a pent-up stream bursting its banks poured out the story of his troubled condition. How she rejoiced in her heart! Simply explaining again the way of salvation, she added: 'Look, we didn't know you were coming tonight, and two relatives are in the bedroom, so while I prepare a bed for you here, I suggest you go out to the barn and tell God what you have told me.'

What followed is best described in his own words: 'I entered the barn, and falling on my knees among the straw prepared for the horses in the morning I began to pray. I well remember the prayer that I offered. It was in Gaelic (I'm so thankful that God understands Gaelic!): "Lord, I know not what to do. I know not how to come, but if You'll take me as I am, I'm coming now." And in less time than I can take to tell it I was gloriously saved kneeling in the straw. I rose from my knees clinging to a simple word of promise: "He that heareth my word, and believeth on Him that sent me, has passed from death unto life." I was saved with God's eternal salvation!'

With the joy of salvation in his heart he went back to the kitchen to tell his mother what had happened. Together they knelt by the dying embers in the hearth and with the flame of love rising within praised God for His mercy. A mother's heart was bursting with gratitude as she cried: 'Oh God, You are still the God who answers prayer.'

Next day an old Sunday School teacher stopped him by the roadside and asked: 'Is it true, what I hear, that you were in the prayer-meeting last night?'

'It is true. You heard right.'

'And why don't you come to Jesus?'

'I did, last night,' was the reply, and then added something which indicated that he was still in the conflict, facing the accusing darts of the devil, 'But I'm not sure whether He accepted me or not.'

But as he testified to the events of the past night, such a flood of joy and assurance swept over him that he had to run behind some bushes and pour out expressions of gratitude and praise to God.

Referring to this incident later he said: 'Never for a moment since have I had the slightest reason to doubt the work that God did in my soul. It was a supernatural experience. A miracle happened!'

He was over the top; Satan's bid for his soul was foiled. The battle was won.

From that moment salvation was real to Duncan Campbell. God became real. It was more than a decision. It was an encounter with the living God. Ever after he could only be satisfied with this note of reality in preaching and experience. His cry was: 'Is God real to you? We are living in a day, particularly in the field of evangelism, when everything is real but God. Organisation, real! Activity, real! Evangelism, real! Decision, real! Yes, even decisions can be real to you without God. Oh, tell me, is God the supreme reality in your experience?'

His fears that there are many who in the hour of decision do not become conscious of a new beginning with God were not without foundation. After a meeting in London, five young nurses came to see him. They told how they had made decisions at a large crusade, and then one of them confessed: 'We went through the mechanics, Mr. Campbell, but we are not changed.'

The test of salvation is in its ethical results and

whether a man is a social outcast or a respectable person, it requires a miracle to re-create a sinner into a devoted, obedient follower of Jesus Christ.

That miracle altered the character and conduct of Duncan Campbell. He had reached 'the crisis of his history' and the course of his life was re-mapped. The pleasures of the dance-hall and worldly popularity had no further place in his thinking. The chairman at the concert had to eat his words for Duncan never 'got over' the constraining power of the Holy Spirit that had taken him from the platform of the world and put him on the road to God.

CHAPTER FOUR

Mobilised

WITH a major battle won in his own inner life, Duncan
soon recognised that his engagement to follow Christ
meant entering upon a life of spiritual warfare with 'the
world, the flesh and the devil'. Jesus Christ had become
the Captain of his salvation and the greatest honour a
man could have was to fight beneath His banner. His
determined energies were immediately channelled in a
new direction.

Blackcrofts became 'Jerusalem' to Duncan Campbell.
Like the early disciples, who changed the course of history
with the explosive news of salvation, he first witnessed to
everyone in his own locality before reaching out to wider
spheres of influence. The Pilgrims continued to conduct
missions in the neighbourhood and with vigour and enthusiasm he threw himself into the task of assisting them by
inviting others to the services and relating the story of
his own encounter with God. While he had never been a
vandal or blasphemer, it still was evident that something
transforming had happened in the life of the young shop-
assistant. His willingness to help the sick and elderly,
and the sincerity of his attitudes and actions, convinced
friends and neighbours of the reality of his conversion.

There is no greater joy than that of soul-winning. Duncan readily endorsed the words of Charles Haddon Spurgeon who said: 'Even if I were utterly selfish, and had no care for anything but my own happiness, I would choose if I might, under God, to be a soul-winner; for never did I know perfect, overflowing, unutterable happiness of the purest and most ennobling order till I first heard of one who had sought and found the Saviour through my means. No young mother ever rejoiced more over her first-born child, no warrior was so exultant over a hard-won victory.'

The first person he had honourable mention in helping to win to the Saviour was his own cousin, Archie. The Pilgrims had moved from the little hall at Alt-na-mara to conduct house-meetings in the home of William Black, a local joiner, who lived in one of the Blackcroft houses. Duncan encouraged them in this mission, watching and praying for souls who needed the Saviour. One cold January day he met Archie and spoke to him about Christ. The words made a deep impression. Archie said: 'I believed in Duncan. His testimony was sincere. I wished I could be like him.' The same night he went to the house-meeting and received Christ. Later he became a school-teacher and still joyfully remembers the day Duncan directed him into a living attachment to the Saviour.

Interest in the Pilgrims' missions increased. Many were brought to Christ as the Holy Spirit worked mightily and meetings were arranged to instruct the young converts. A barn was cleaned and whitewashed for the purpose.

Meantime, a lady who lived in one of the local crofts decided to move to Glasgow and asked her brother in Portuairk, Ardnamurchan, if he would like to have the

croft. So Archibald Gray and his wife Margaret, with
their young family, agreed to live at Blackcrofts. To
finalise the arrangement, Archie came for a week bringing
his youngest daughter, Shona, to stay with her aunt until
the move was completed.

A local Christian took the lassie to the meeting one
evening and the following night she returned with her
aunt. One of the Pilgrims had taken ill and a Mr. Wallace
was assisting. As he spoke Shona recalled the prayers of
her parents and especially the death of a schoolfriend
which had caused her to think seriously about eternity.
These impressions culminated in a crisis as she sat in
the barn. A shy nature prevented her from remaining
behind, as those concerned were invited to do, but at the
door Mr. Wallace placed a hand on her shoulder and
gently asked: 'Have you given your life to the Lord yet?'

'Oh, but she was brought up in a good Christian
home,' her aunt interrupted, before the girl had time to
reply.

This objection only intensified the conviction that she
was still unprepared for eternity, and she exclaimed:
'Oh, no, auntie, I'm still not saved.'

'And wouldn't you like to give your life to the Lord
tonight?' Mr. Wallace asked.

'Yes, indeed.'

On her knees in the barn, with an old man of seventy
years also seeking peace, she committed her life to Christ.

Turning at the door that night she noticed a young lad
with red hair standing like a sentinel outside, rejoicing
that others were seeking the Saviour.

But as he watched her leave the barn there was more
than casual interest kindled in his heart toward the
dark-haired newcomer to Blackcrofts. Next day when
she called at the shop with her aunt and was introduced

to him, his reply was very deliberate: 'Yes, I saw her last night.' With usual determination he had already made up his mind that one day she would be his wife!

Some respectable church folk were once upset when Duncan proclaimed: 'What the world needs to see is God in dungarees!' He was emphasising the importance of the life of God in the Christian being worked out in everyday employment and not merely at church on Sunday. When he himself wore a shop-coat he proved his point. All who patronised MacSwan's grocery business in Connel Ferry village knew what the young assistant stood for. The boss complained: 'If you don't stop preaching to the customers I'll have to get someone to take your place.'

'Then you must look for a new assistant,' was Duncan's response. At the same time no one was more pleased with his honesty and sincerity than his employer. He was an elder in the church, though not a very consistent one, as the following incident seems to illustrate.

Outside the shop each evening a few ex-servicemen gathered with the lads of the village and 'Duncie Doo', the local wit. One evening as the grocer was leaving the shop an old Christian by the name of Corson passed by on his way from the prayer meeting. The grocer turned to Duncie Doo, hoping for some fun at the old gentleman's expense: 'I wonder, Duncie, does the devil ever torment old Corson?'

The opportunity was too good to miss.

'I'm surprised at ye,' replied Duncie slyly. 'I'm surprised at ye, an elder in the Kirk an' no' kenin' anything aboot it! It's the likes o' him he does torment. He kens he's got you an' me already!'

Duncan Campbell refused to believe in the religion of anyone who was too preoccupied to attend a prayer-meeting. The place of prayer was the test of a man's

spiritual life. When a man is born again and the Spirit
of God dwells within him, desires and aspirations are
born that find expression in prayer. He also gauged the
spiritual life of a church with the same measuring rod.
The number attending the prayer-meeting is more
important than the size of the Sunday morning congregation.

The term 'worldly Christian' was anathema to him.
He was a total abstainer and hated smoking and dancing.
He never lost an opportunity to voice his opinion on
these and other worldly issues, yet one never received
the impression that he was being narrow and repressive.
When in the company of those who did indulge, he
created no feeling of moral superiority. When visiting a
young man who worked as a blender in a whisky business
he was offered a glass to embarrass him into leaving
quickly. But Duncan calmly replied: 'No thank you. I
don't touch it, but what I would like is a good cup of tea.'

His warm-hearted manner disarmed the young fellow
completely. 'He's not such a bad sort after all,' he
thought, and the cup of tea was provided, followed by a
lengthy and profitable conversation.

In the school of experience Duncan learned early
the price of betraying principles and compromising with
what he had formerly disowned. Unmoved by the sneers
of the world, he discovered that there are more subtle
snares to tempt the Christian soldier to soften.

He stopped playing the bagpipes after he was converted feeling that the associations with this pleasure
would be a hindrance to spiritual progress. One day
visitors arrived and his sister, proud of his former
performances, pestered him to play. He yielded and
picking up the pipes started on *The Barren Rocks of Aden*.
Immediately the light within went out. Peace and joy

fled from him. Pride had welled up in his heart and
grieved the Lord. Throwing down the instrument he was
about to leave, when another sister came in. She had
been working outside and hearing the music thought:
'That's Duncan playing.' Unknown to others she was
under conviction of sin and, previously impressed by
Duncan's bold witness, was seriously considering the cost
of following Christ. She felt disappointed that he seemed
to be returning to his old pleasures and with a questioning
look asked: 'Does Christ not satisfy?'

A knife thrust could not have been more painful.
His distress was aggravated tenfold, and he ran from the
house in agony of spirit.

All day he mourned his defeat. Toward evening he
wandered dejectedly to the home of Mrs. Gray, a 'mother
in Israel', to whom he was deeply attached and poured
out the story of his smitten conscience: 'I've let the Lord
down today.'

If he was looking for sympathy in his misery he was
disappointed. The wise woman recognised that God was
using this issue to test his submission and loyalty; the
chastening hand of the Lord upon him would bring
lessons in obedience that would be a benefit in years to
come. She felt deeply for the young offender but offered
no false comfort. 'Just leave it with the Lord and if you
are a child of God you will come back with many stripes!'
was her plain advice.

He was knocked down but not knocked out! Incidents
like these educated him in the tactics of the enemy and
every opportunity to proclaim Christ was eagerly grasped.

When the Pilgrims left the district the battle continued.
A weekly Prayer Union meeting was started in
Matheson's barn and, with 'a correspondence fixed with
heaven', business was transacted on behalf of those who

were still unsaved. And the matter didn't end there. The young folk mobilised to spread the gospel, Meetings were held in barns and homes over a wide area. Sandy Matheson, who had been converted when the Pilgrims were there, started to preach. He was older than the others and encouraged the younger recruits. Often they walked as far as seven miles to meetings, singing hymns on the way. During the summer they reinforced the team of Pilgrims on an open-air campaign in Oban, and always at the centre of things was the former piper, already showing characteristics that singled him out as a future leader.

His mother encouraged this activity. On Sabbath afternoons she took him with her to visit those unable to attend church. After singing together, Duncan would read and pray, bringing light and comfort to needy hearts. But he was by no means a mature saint. He was often impatient with those who were not so active or sympathetic to his robust ways. An impetuous streak on more than one occasion led him to act without due caution or consideration. But he was teachable and listened readily to the advice of others.

One incident he never forgot. He was disappointed that the minister and members of his father's church had not given whole-hearted support to the Pilgrims. Some were critical of the converts. Nor was the message of salvation being explained with sufficient clarity, and for him the Church was too lax in communion. Why continue to attend? Better to join the other local church where the Rev. D. M. Cameron had been such a help to the Pilgrims. He voiced his opinions in vehement tones to his mother. She sympathised with his sentiments but sought to steady his stormy spirit. 'Son, if God has lit a lamp in your life, let it shine in the darkness.'

He stayed where he was, but satisfied his spiritual hunger at the Prayer Union, with occasional visits to Mr. Cameron. Patience had its reward years later when the minister with whom he had been disappointed, sent for him, desiring his help and prayers, confessing his unfaithfulness and saying how much it meant to him that Duncan had remained in the church.

The fight had begun in earnest at 'Jerusalem' and from there he was soon to be transferred to another battlefield, very different from the wild beauty of the lochs and glens and ancient hills of Argyll.

CHAPTER FIVE

'Blood and Mud'

'BLOOD AND MUD! Blood and mud! The Campaign of the mud!' was how David Lloyd George, the British Prime Minister, described the 1917 Flanders Campaign. Passchendaele Ridge was the centre of this Allied offensive that sparked off the most savage, appalling bloodbath of the Great War.

The Ridge itself was one of a series of faint rises on the vast Flanders plain where rivers and canals merged on low-lying flats to flow slowly and silently into the English Channel. Small woods and farm-houses were the only landmarks discernible across the otherwise feature-less expanse.

Even these were now gone. Incessant shell-fire had obliterated every dwelling place; woods were levelled to resemble a few scarred and broken poles, stuck aimlessly into the ground; the village of Passchendaele had vanished, reduced to a heap of rubble, but the rubble on the ridge was still a strategic military treasure coveted by the advancing forces.

Advance was slow. The Germans were well entrenched in reinforced 'pillboxes'. But the chief enemy was mud. Steady rain had fallen, and canals torn open by months of

shelling had churned the battlefield into a quagmire.
Trenches and shell-craters oozed with slimy, green water
and molasses-like mud. Men seeking refuge in these
from enemy fire often perished in the foul smelling
liquid.

'No battle was ever fought under such conditions,'
wrote General Gough. Wave after wave of men struggled
through the gluey swamp in the face of the most terrible
machine-gun fire ever directed against soldiers.
Thousands fell in every attack. Others took their place.
To advance four-and-a-half miles took four months
and cost half-a-million casualties.

In the first assault on Passchendaele Ridge 13,000
were slaughtered in a few hours. The dead littered the
ground, white teeth showing on brown, stricken faces.
The wounded groaned, or cried out with the pain of
shattered limbs. Others with shattered minds wandered
aimlessly, crying, giggling, or muttering incoherently, no
longer able to defend themselves.

Somewhere in the midst of this sea of mud and human
carnage a machine-gunner crouched behind his weapon.
He was only a lad, still in his late teens, but according to
the War Office old enough to fight, and die if need be.
It was a miracle that he was still alive. The life expectancy
of a machine-gunner in battle on the Western Front was
computed at thirty minutes!

Lying there, his mind went back to the peaceful shores
of Loch Etive and the home from which he had been
rudely snatched. His brother, John, had been conscripted
when hostilities commenced, and was serving in Mesopo-
tamia. The war had dragged on and two years later his
turn had come.

Enlisting with the Argyll and Sutherland Highlanders,
he was sent to the regimental headquarters at Stirling

Castle for 'square-bashing', and to be trained in the art of killing men, before reaching the front line.

Duncan respected the views of fellow Christians who objected to this distasteful business on conscientious grounds, but he was not a pacifist. Admonished by a conscientious objector for participating, he replied that during his term of service he suffered no twinge of conscience.

'You have no conscience,' was the dry reply.

War was no less horrible and repulsive to him than to anyone else, but when choosing between war and the tyranny of aggression, he regarded the former as the lesser of two evils.

Mother would be praying for them. Standing outside the croft with a far-away look that betrayed her communion with another world, or kneeling in the barn she waited patiently and prayed constantly. They would come home; of that she was sure. To them it seemed unlikely.

Then there was the girl he had left behind. From his pocket he drew again the photograph she had given him. It strengthened him to think of her. In the barrack room the boys had poked fun at him: 'Oh, c'mon Campbell, why don't you join us for a night out?'

There were many invitations to abandon faith and discard principles, but showing them the photograph he simply said he would rather be faithful to her. It amused him to remember how on one occasion she cost him a hard-earned stripe when he overstayed his leave to see her.

Their last parting was still vivid in his mind. They had just been to the Highland Mission in Glasgow with his sister. Duncan MacColl, the unconventional founder and superintendent of the Mission, also a native of Benderloch, spotted the young soldier and enlisted him for active service immediately. Bounding back to the platform he announced: 'There's a young man here who is leaving tonight for Alnwick, on his way to France. He's going to testify for his Saviour.'

Duncan described again his encounter with God and the progress he had made. Requesting the prayers of God's people, he then asked if he could sing a hymn. He sang:

> Hold Thou my hand! so weak I am, and helpless,
> I dare not take one step without Thy aid;
> Hold Thou my hand! for then, O loving Saviour,
> No dread of ill shall make my soul afraid.

A quick cup of tea after the meeting and they left for the station, singing hymns as they walked.

Would he ever see them again? Hundreds were being cut down around him. The chatter of machine-guns, the 'wham' of shells, and the cries of the wounded were a daily noise in his ears. What chance did he have? In desperation, he cried out: 'Oh God, get me out of here and I will serve You with my whole heart'—a promise he never forgot.

Before that prayer was answered there were other lessons to learn in this bitter and dangerous school of experience.

Knowledge was gained through experience. The battle-field, for example, taught Duncan the value of teamwork. They were not fighting to settle private quarrels. Each soldier was part of an army with one aim in view. Negligence on the part of one could cause others to suffer. Duncan learned this as a machine-gunner. Two men operated each gun. As a Number One gunner his task was to assemble and fire the weapon, to provide covering fire for the advancing infantry. His partner was to check and feed the belts of ammunition into the gun. During heavy fighting he once saw a man fail to check his ammunition properly. The belt twisted and the gun stuck. Those relying on them for cover were mown down like corn before the reaper.

From this he appreciated how essential it was to work in harmony in the body of Christ. If one member suffers, all suffer. He recognised his responsibility spiritually for souls. His every moral and spiritual victory would be a triumph for someone else, but if he lost touch with God, others with whom he lived and worked would also suffer loss.

The brevity of life, the folly of neglecting the soul and being unprepared for death and judgment were deeply etched upon his thinking at the front line. Death-bed repentance was common, but too often insincere.

In the pitched battles, where attackers and attacked often changed position, casualties among junior officers were high. Corporals and even privates had to take command of platoons. Duncan found himself in charge of a platoon before a particularly fierce battle. The assault was going to be costly; few would be coming back. Five other sergeants, knowing he was a Christian, asked him to pray with them and explain the way of salvation. All professed to receive Christ.

The battle was a bloody one. As expected, few returned. Then word reached him that two of the five had been spared. Immediately he sent a messenger inviting them to join in prayer to thank God for deliverance. The messenger found them celebrating with the rum rations and the blunt message carried back was: 'Tell Campbell and his prayer-meeting to go to hell!'

Said Duncan afterwards: 'God is not unwilling to show mercy at the eleventh hour, witness the dying thief; but

I fear that in too many cases there is little genuine desire for mercy.'

Life was cheap on the Western Front. Retreat was frowned upon even when a position became intolerable. Duncan once risked a court martial by 'staking rifle' to bring his men back from certain death. He believed the adage that 'he who fights and runs away, lives to fight another day'. A senior officer didn't agree but severely reprimanded him and then asked: 'Where's your gun?'

'I left it behind to get the men out. We had to run for our lives.'

'To hell with your lives! Did you take the breach out?'

'No.'

'Go back and get it, or you're a corpse!'

Guns were more important than men.

But the finest lesson Duncan learned in France was that the possibilities of advance with God could never be exhausted, even in the blackest situation. The spiritual conflict was equally fierce, but behind the clouds that sometimes shadowed his spirit was the unerring hand of God, leading him to see the deeper sin of his own heart and to know a fuller experience of the power of Christ to forgive and cleanse. With his eye upon a sovereign Saviour, in the darkest hour, he

> 'Never doubted clouds would break, never dreamed
> Tho' right were worsted, wrong would triumph,
> Held we fall to rise—are baffled to fight better . . .'
>   Robert Browning.

CHAPTER SIX

Deliverance

GOD answered the prayers of Duncan's mother and his own desperate cry for deliverance by precipitating a spiritual crisis in his life. It was in exit from the battlefield that he experienced the second major unheaval in his Christian life.

Army life was a startling contrast to the sheltered upbringing he had enjoyed. Suddenly thrust into the company of godless men who laughed at religion and gloried in sin, he was frequently ridiculed and exposed to temptations unknown before.

The doctrine of total depravity, teaching that there is in the heart of man the seed of every conceivable sin, was demonstrated practically for him in the Army. The war provided an opportunity for many to cut loose from the restraints of childhood discipline and accepted, social standards. Drunkenness and immorality abounded.

He saw the bestiality of which man is capable, when unrestrained by the preventing grace of God. To satisfy the cravings of untethered nature men stooped below animal level. One sight in particular repelled him. A beer barrel had been smashed and the contents spilled on the ground. Rather than lose their rations a group of men went on their hands and knees to drink it out of mud that was saturated with human blood. To see men openly and unashamedly live in vice was a disturbing experience for a teenage lad recruited from a God-fearing community.

But he was even more distressed to find that when the initial shock of this environment subsided, a principle of evil was also working within himself, threatening to shipwreck faith and bring him into bondage to the very sins he abhorred in others. His mind was bombarded with foul suggestions; impure thoughts and desires coursing through his nature disturbed him during those long months.

Mercifully preserved from gross sin, he must have been guilty of at least one venial offence against his conscience. An old Seaforth Highlander declares that he heard him play the pipes again in France!

Soon the depravity of his heart became unbearable. Not since conversion had he experienced such inner conflict. He had received Christ and become a partaker of his new nature; he was 'born again' and wanted to obey and follow the Saviour, but another law was striving within, at war with the life of Christ, threatening to land him in despair.

In his wretchedness he cried to God. Again and again falling on his knees in the trenches he asked God to deliver him and keep him from an open betrayal of Christ, realising then, as throughout the remainder of his life, that he could not keep himself, not for five minutes. The prayer of David in distress and danger when oppressed by his enemies became Duncan's lifelong prayer: 'Hold up my goings in thy paths, that my footsteps slip not' (Ps.17:5).

The conditions around where men slithered and slipped in the mud, or tried desperately to keep their heads above water in a trench, reflected his own moral and spiritual battle. His cry for deliverance from the corruption around was eclipsed by the cry for deliverance from the enemy within. Like the Psalmist he felt he was sinking in deep mire where there is no standing, that he was come into deep waters where the floods overflowed him, and in his extremity groaned: 'I am weary of my crying; my throat is dried; mine eyes fail while I wait for my God' (Ps.69:3).

He waited for God and the moment of deliverance came.

The spring had come and with it the long anticipated German counter-offensive; the Allies were swept off Passchendaele Ridge. Their costly occupation had afforded only a few months of unsettled accommodation for the winter. Now they were in full retreat.

Meantime word had reached the military authorities that the machine-gunner in the trenches had been reared on a farm and was acquainted with horses. Men were needed in the Cavalry Corps. It was suggested (one of those Army suggestions that leaves little option) that he should attach himself to a Cavalry division. Thus he found himself outside Amiens in April, 1918, engaged in one of the last major cavalry charges of the British Army.

They plunged into the fray but were no match for the advancing forces. Within minutes the new trooper had his horse shot from under him and lay severely wounded. The dead and dying were all around with riderless horses running wild among the bodies.

Blood flowed from his wounds and feeling he was dying, a sense of unfitness enveloped him. He rejoiced that he was accepted by God on the merits of Christ's death alone, but was distressed at the thought of going to meet the Saviour with such inner depravity. A verse from the Bible repeatedly gripped him: 'Without holiness no man shall see the Lord.'

Grieved that he had accomplished so little for the Saviour, he recalled a hymn often sung at family worship: 'Must I go and empty-handed, must I meet my Saviour so?' It seemed that was how he was now going to meet Him.

Just then a second charge was ordered out and the men of the Canadian Horse urged their steeds across the debris of men and animals left by the former attack. There was no time yet to attend to dead and wounded.

As the charge flew past, a horse's hoof struck Duncan in the spine. He groaned. That groan saved his life.

The Canadians cleared the heights, giving a brief breathing-space to the hard-pressed divisions. Returning from the charge, the trooper whose horse had struck Duncan came right back to where he lay. The groan had registered in his mind constraining him to return. Picking up the wounded man, he threw him across his horse, and galloped to the nearest Casualty Clearing Station.

Duncan was now weak from loss of blood and could see little hope of life, but he was still more concerned about the state of his soul. Then the prayer of Robert Murray McCheyne, which he had often heard his father pray, flashed into his mind: 'Lord, make me as holy as a saved sinner can be.'

Lying on the horse's back, persuaded that he was dying, Duncan prayed it again in an agony of earnestness. Instantly the power of God possessed him. Like a purging fire the Holy Spirit swept through his personality, bringing cleansing and renewal until 'at that moment I felt as pure as an angel'. The consciousness of God was so real that he concluded he was going straight to heaven.

But God had other work for him to do and this revolutionary experience was preparation for it. Duncan was not concerned about tying any particular theological label to his new meeting with God. Sometimes he referred to it as the 'baptism of the Holy Ghost', 'the fullness of the Holy Spirit' or an experience of 'full salvation'. The terms were unimportant; it was the ethical and practical outcome that mattered.

The sequel to this Divine visitation gave him his first taste of the supernatural work that can accompany the reviving touch of the Spirit of God upon His people. From that moment revival became a glorious possibility; something to live for, to work for, and to pray for.

At the Casualty Clearing Station a skeleton staff was operating. The place was prepared for evacuation. He was carried in on a stretcher and placed among the other wounded. They were mainly Canadian troopers, waiting to be transferred by ambulance to the nearest hospital.

A nurse in the Station was also from the Highlands. When the newcomer arrived, she came to his bedside and began to sing in Gaelic the words of Cowper's hymn:

> There is a fountain filled with blood
> Drawn from Immanuel's veins.

Already in an ecstasy of joy, his heart bubbled over with praise to God. He began to quote, also in Gaelic, the Scottish metrical version of the 103rd Psalm. It is doubtful if any of the men around understood a word of the language he was speaking, but a stillness came over the ward and the awareness of God captured the consciousness of each one. Within minutes conviction of sin laid hold of them and at least seven Canadians trusted Christ. Before being lifted from the Station Duncan heard these men testify to what happened in that moment of miracle. The reality of God's presence, through the praise of His servant, had so charged the atmosphere with the fear of God that these men were convinced of their sin and gloriously converted.

Duncan realised then, that while our present surroundings, comfortable or adverse, are the field in which we fight the battles of faith, it is in the spiritual realm that we win. This is the secret of supernatural power. He described the early Christians, in the midst of a hostile environment, as being spiritually located in the Lord; their lives were 'hid with Christ in God', therefore they carried about with them a private atmosphere, one that was not of Asia Minor but of heaven.

A new thirst for God, a thirst for revival, a thirst to see repeated manifestations of God's saving power, took hold of Duncan Campbell as he left an earthly battlefield, to devote himself to the spiritual war from which there is no discharge.

CHAPTER SEVEN

Trials and Triumphs of Training

On discharge from hospital in Perth, where he had been taken, Duncan was demobilised. Arriving at Black-crofts he ran into the house, threw his army bonnet across the room and exclaimed: 'I'm finished with you now!'

His mother was waiting to welcome him, rejoicing that God had answered prayer.

Days of recuperation among his native hills brought fresh vigour to his body and afforded many hours of delightful fellowship with God. Roaming the moors, listening to the mountain streams, and gazing across the loch to the peaks of Cruachan was excellent therapy; the peaceful atmosphere and clean mountain air seemed to wash over his mind and spirit with healing calm.

When the family gathered around the fire in the evening he would relate stories of the war in Europe. Highlanders are inveterate story-tellers. Until the appearance of television neighbours assembled almost nightly in one or other of the crofts for a *ceilidh*. Tales of history, romance and folklore were told and retold until even the children were quite adept in the use of descriptive speech. Duncan had mastered this art and regaled his listeners with scenes from the battlefield, so vivid and dramatic, that it seemed the bogs of Benderloch became the trenches of Flanders and the Germans were already advancing over Ben Lora!

It was the cherished hope of Scottish parents in those days to have a son in the church, and Duncan's parents were anxious to have his education furthered with a view to entering the ministry when fully recovered from his injuries. Duncan could see no sense in it. Ridiculous! Why waste five or six years studying when he could be doing something practical for God? Had God not saved seven souls in the Casualty Clearing Station without a word being spoken to them? Could He not do it again? The Holy Spirit was sovereign in the work of salvation.

He moderated his views on the worth of education later, but these were his arguments then, and, seeing his determination to get on with the job, his parents were happy to leave him to his own leadings.

With their permission, and particularly the encouragement of his mother, he left the farm to go out into the villages and country districts of Argyllshire 'just to talk about Jesus'. Without attempting to preach, he read from the Scriptures and prayed in the homes visited, adding the story of his own conversion. The uncommon earnestness and sincerity of these 'kitchen devotions' moved many God-ward.

Gaelic was his native language. Its reputation for being one of the most expressive languages in the world extremely suits the presentation of the gospel. A Highland friend writes that to Duncan nothing could be compared with the language of his boyhood—and no amount of teasing would change his mind on this issue!

Sometimes he remarked that it was the language of heaven! A speaker who shared the ministry with him during a convention in Ireland heard this comment and quipped: 'It must be, it's like nothing on earth!'

But Duncan wasn't browbeaten. To clarify the meaning of a verse of Scripture to his English-speaking audience he translated from the Gaelic version of the Bible, adding with a smile: 'It's much nearer the original than your English version!'

The flush of youthful enthusiasm sometimes yields to the teaching of experience where advice fails to influence. The would-be evangelist after battling alone for a while decided there was merit in his parents' suggestion of further preparation and that it was with some reason that Jesus sent His disciples out in twos.

He saw the value of a period of training and study, but still rejected the idea of more than half-a-decade of bookwork in order to preach. It was natural to feel drawn towards the work of the Faith Mission. The workers went out in pairs engaging in the type of rural evangelism to which he was inclined. He could train there, but would he be sent back to work in his beloved Highlands?

Should he apply? Was this God's leading, or mere natural affection for the Pilgrims and the work that had been the means of his conversion? Duncan never suffered long from indecision. With a mind at rest that he was doing God's will, he made application, was accepted, packed his case and left for Edinburgh.

John George Govan had moved the headquarters of the Mission from the west of Scotland to its historic capital, where a large grey-stoned building overlooking the Firth of Forth had been gifted to the Mission to use as a

Training Home where young people could be equipped for mission-work at home and abroad.

In 1919 the basic training period was of nine months duration—short, but intensive and effective. Mr. Govan was anxious to send out those who could endure hardness as good soldiers of Jesus Christ. Discipline was the watch-word, disentanglement from all unnecessary affairs was expected of each one, and cheerful diligence in executing duties assigned.

Practical work was no burden to the Highland student, but lectures and study were a problem due to his meagre education and limited knowledge of English. More than once Mr. Govan remarked: 'Brother Campbell, I some-times wonder if you will ever make a Pilgrim!' But with typical determination, passionate love for God, and zeal to win souls, Duncan won through.

Faith was thoroughly tested in training. When it seemed that prayer for his fees was going unanswered Duncan sought the Chief in distress. But God had gone before, and Mr. Govan was able to tell him: 'The Lord has provided in His own way.' God had touched the heart of a wealthy, Christian lady, who had been a customer in the shop where Duncan had worked, to send financial help direct to Mr. Govan.

Visiting ministers lectured to the students on a variety of subjects but it was Mr. Govan's own lectures which impressed Duncan most. These were no dry-as-dust sessions for acquiring theological facts and statistics. They were warm, life-giving and vibrant with power.

Mr. Govan was extremely sensitive to spiritual atmos-phere. He encouraged the students to cultivate this faculty. None did so more than Duncan Campbell. One day Mr. Govan, before commencing a lecture, announced the hymn:

Here from the world we turn,
    Jesus to seek;
Here may His loving voice
    Graciously speak!
Jesus our dearest Friend,
While at Thy feet we bend,
Oh, let Thy smile descend!
    'Tis Thee we seek.

Before they could start singing, a Highland boy
quietly stood to his feet and said: 'Mr. Govan, He *is* my
dearest Friend.'

The effect was startling! The sentiment of that simple
statement was infectious and challenging. A swelling tide
of desire for God swept through those present. Spontaneously they went on their knees and remained in prayer
for hours. The lecture was forgotten. Mr. Govan recognised that such a meeting with God would accomplish
more to equip these lives for service than lectures could
ever do.

Mr. and Mrs. Govan were always glad to see Highland
students coming to the Training Home, especially those
with a knowledge of Gaelic. They took an interest in
Duncan and endeavoured to help him, encouraging his
desire to be a soul-winner and at the same time seeking to
mellow his impulsive ways. This trait came out strongly
one day when someone told him he was proud of his
beautiful, red, curly hair. 'You must spend more time in
front of the mirror than you do on your knees, Duncan!'
That was just too much! He would prove his curls were no
idol. Off he went to the barber and came back with a
jail-cut! His curls never grew again.

'Tiny' Towler was a wee pint-sized Welsh girl, also in
training. One day Duncan met her on the stairs labouring

under a pile of rugs she was taking out to shake. Communication between male and female students was then restricted to conversation at meal times, but undaunted by rules and regulations Duncan relieved Tiny of her burden, carried it down, and faced a mild reprimand afterwards. That was Duncan the student—not too studious, but thoughtful, and keen to help.

Another day he unwittingly breached the communication lines by visiting one of the girls who had taken ill. Accustomed to reserving Sunday afternoons to visit the sick with his mother, he made his way to the Sisters' quarters to read and pray with the patient. The 'law of the Medes and Persians' was broken! He was immediately reported to 'the Chief' who lightheartedly forgave the offender.

Another amusing incident during training days was more difficult to pass off. The offended was less disposed to forgive. It happened in the dental surgery. Missionary candidates needed some dental 'know-how' in order to handle emergencies on isolated mission stations. So some of the students attended the Dispensary of the Edinburgh Medical Missionary Society. Duncan went too, to watch the process of tooth extraction.

The dentist, a former missionary, was a kindly man who took an interest in the students. They were only to watch, but one day an old woman was having some teeth pulled and he offered Duncan the forceps. Following careful instructions, Duncan soon had the offending molar in the tray. Simple! The dentist commended the effort, and on the next visit invited him to try again. This time the patient was a big Irish navvy in a hurry to get relief from a burning toothache. It is fatal to forget that the teeth of a strong working-man are more firmly rooted than those of an elderly woman. But that's what happened.

Push! Twist! Pull! That's what he was told, but this
time it was not so simple! The forceps slipped and nipped
the navvy's tongue. He jumped to his feet, roaring with
pain and amid unprintable exclamations and a few invoc-
ations to the Virgin Mary and various saints outlined what
he would do with the head of the amateur. The dentist
eventually pacified him and pulled the tooth, but that day
Duncan severed diplomatic relations with dental surgery!

Visiting homes, distributing literature, and witnessing
in the public houses, or to the down-and-outs in lodging
houses, were some of the outreach activities connected
with training, but open-air meetings were Duncan's
favourite. His short word in Gaelic drew numbers of
passing Highlanders who worked in the capital to hear
the gospel. Mrs. Govan suggested he should play hymn-
tunes on the bagpipes at the open-airs. 'If they use harps
in heaven, why not use bagpipes here?' she asked. That
sounded like sacrilege to Duncan; he wouldn't hear
of it!

On Sunday evenings the students joined other Mission
personnel for open-air witness at Haymarket, which
was a quiet junction of streets in those days, and a good
stand for an open-air meeting. One showery evening
Duncan told how the Lord had saved him and concluded
with a few simple comments on the saving gaze of faith
from the verse: 'Look unto me, and be ye saved, all the
ends of the earth,' when a young woman approached him.
While the others sang: 'There is life for a look at the
crucified One,' she told her story. It was the oft-repeated
tragedy of city life. Brought up in a good home, but
attracted by the promise of pleasure and success, she
left to seek adventure. Difficult times, wrong company
and bad habits followed, until she was forced to earn her
living on the streets. Now, ashamed to go home, and

afraid to meet God, she wept bitterly, hardly wanting to live and not daring to die.

With tears of repentance she asked: 'Can Christ do for me what He has done for you?'

'Are you in earnest?' Duncan inquired.

'Yes, indeed.'

'Then will you kneel with me here and ask Christ to save you now?'

She nodded. Instinctively he pulled off his coat and placed it on the wet cobblestones. The young woman called upon the Lord, and looking in faith to the Cross of Jesus saw her sins forgiven and removed for ever.

She became a doctor's wife and lived for many years to prove the genuineness of her conversion, rearing her family for God through a consistent testimony to the miracle that took place on the cobblestones.

The world acclaimed the courtesy of Sir Walter Raleigh when he laid his cloak on the ground for his Queen to step from her carriage. History books have not recorded the open-air meeting at Haymarket, but what acclamation there must have been in heaven when a young student cast his coat on the cobblestones to pave the way for the King of kings to take up His residence in the renewed life.

Nine months quickly passed and the richer for his experiences in the fellowship of the Training Home, Duncan was eager to step out into the battlefield again to prepare the way of the Lord in other lives. He had become more acquainted with his Captain, gained a new knowledge of the tactics of the enemy and learned to use more effectively the equipment provided for spiritual warfare.

CHAPTER EIGHT

Into Battle

THE final term brought great excitement at the Training Home. Hopes and fears like the surge of the tide ebbed and flowed through the hearts of the students as they awaited exam results and the announcement of mission locations. Duncan was 'keyed up', impatient to know his appointment.

Mr. Govan went down the list: 'North Irish District—Brother Campbell!'

'Oh, no, it can't be!' Like Job, the thing which he greatly feared was come upon him. Disappointment overwhelmed him; not getting back to the Highlands after all his hopes and prayers—and hints!

'The Irish were more longsuffering with poor preachers —that's why they sent me there,' he commented later. More likely it was because they appreciated better his fighting spirit.

An old Highland revivalist, Rev. D. T. MacKay, Tiree, used to say: 'If ye canna rouse the Lord's people, rouse the devil!' The Pilgrims did both during the summer and autumn of 1920 in Co. Antrim. They preached in a garage, and when local Christians were stirred to join them in prayer, lives and homes were transformed. A

father and son in one family, a mother and son in
another, and a husband and wife, one a Roman Catholic
and the other a Protestant, were among those seeking
Christ.

Opposition mounted when they went to the school in
Ballybogey. Hooligans turned out to disturb the meetings.
One day a lady marched up to their lodgings demanding
to see the evangelists. She heaped threats upon them for
causing a sensation in the community, and if the mission
did not close within a few days she would have them put
into the hands of the police! They praised God and carried on. Opposition was a sign of Divine activity, and soon
souls were being saved. For six weeks they continued and
when the mission did close the school was too small to
accommodate the people.

A farmer offered his barn for the next mission but
before they could start a letter arrived from Edinburgh
asking Duncan to return to Scotland immediately to work
in Argyllshire. He was delighted. His former desire had
come to pass. Also differences of temperament and
spiritual outlook had created difficulties with his fellow-
worker in Ireland, and he was glad of the change.

The work of missions, according to a missionary
strategist, consists largely in four things to do: contact,
evangelise, organise and instruct. This was the simple
pattern that Duncan and his fellow Pilgrims followed in
the villages of Argyllshire and parts of Inverness-shire
during the next five years.

To establish contact with people in remote, isolated
communities involved long walks, wet clothes, and tired
limbs, but the passion to take the gospel to every creature
made personal sacrifices and physical discomfort a light
burden. 'You must win the people to yourself first,
before you can win them for the Lord,' Duncan insisted.

'And the way to achieve this is by a practical demonstration of kindness and godliness.'

In one community the crofters were busy trying to rescue a late harvest and had little time to come to the meetings. Duncan immediately halted the mission for a week, took off his coat and joined them in the fields helping to cut and stook the corn. When the meetings resumed, the contacts in the cornfield flocked to hear this young fellow who practised what he preached.

Another day, returning to a village where they had been regarded with suspicious courtesy they passed an old tinker woman weighed down with a heavy assortment of pots and pans and other 'tinker ware'. Duncan's companion approached her: 'Can I carry your burden ma'am?' Gratefully the *cailleach* (old lady) handed her load to the Pilgrims who carried it three miles to the village. News of this kind act spread quickly among the people, removing prejudice and softening hearts to receive the Word of life.

God's greatest gift to any generation is not a major breakthrough in science or technology which makes life more easy and prosperous; it is a man with the voice of eternity within calling his fellow-men from paths of selfishness to find satisfaction in God. When Robert Leighton was accused by his ministerial colleagues of not speaking sufficiently to the political and social issues of his day he calmly replied: 'Gentlemen, when so many are speaking to the times, permit one poor brother to speak for eternity.'

Duncan Campbell was a spokesman for eternity. 'We are the ambassadors of eternity in the courts of time, and it is our business to permeate the courts of time with the atmosphere of eternity,' he quoted.

On the doorstep, the street corner, or in the church he used plainness of speech to remove false hopes and show the terrible consequences of sin before pointing men and women to the Saviour. Triflers with truth were silenced unsparingly. A rather self-righteous woman told him she didn't need him to preach to her—she had been through the Bible herself! 'Perhaps so, madam,' he quietly replied, 'but have you allowed the Bible to go through you?' At an open-air meeting in Ballachulish an arrogant young fellow began to mock. Quick as a flash, Duncan turned and rebuked him with solemn effect: 'Young man, your head won't be so high, and your speech won't be so bold when the waves of death are lapping the shores of your body.'

The Island of Mull was the Pilgrims' first battle-ground after Duncan returned from Ireland. They left Oban in the *Lochinvar*, known locally as the 'Coffee Pot', and chugged into Tobermory Bay as the sun was setting. A treasure hunt was causing excitement when they arrived. An effort was being made to recover some gold from a vessel of the Spanish Armada which had been sunk off the coast of Mull in the days of Elizabeth I. But the Pilgrims were more concerned about living treasure, souls that would shine as jewels in the diadem of their Redeemer.

The first convert was a rough diamond; a cantankerous woman who owned the papershop, and 'blew her top' each time the boat came in, when everyone wanted the latest edition at once.

The second was a young girl who attended the meetings and saw her need, but wondered if salvation would really work out if she received Christ by faith. She decided to hide herself and watch the woman from the papershop next time the boat came. If she 'hit the roof' then there was nothing to it; if she remained calm then something real must have happened.

The papers arrived. As usual everyone clamoured into the little store, shouting and gesticulating; but instead of the usual explosion of verbal abuse upon her undisciplined patrons there was courtesy and kindness. The girl left her hiding place, went to the meeting and committed her life to Christ.

Crowds packed the churches and schools in which the Pilgrims preached in different villages; the Spirit of God worked mightily in the meetings, and out of them. A school-teacher out cycling one day was so convicted of her sin that she had to dismount and kneel by the roadside to seek the Lord.

The devil was roused! The publicans especially were bitterly opposed. Trade was beginning to fail, so they hired a man to speak against the Pilgrims and disrupt the meetings. This fellow spread the story that Campbell and he recently unloaded a cargo of lime from the *Star of Hope* in Loch Nell and afterwards drank a bottle of whisky between them! A bold indictment against someone who never drank anything stronger than orange juice.

The same man appeared in the meeting one night wearing an outsize coat. As Duncan was praying, instead of the usual 'Amens' there was a sudden 'Quack, quack; quack, quack,' and two ducks which he had brought in under his coat waddled down the aisle!

In another meeting a young woman came to the front of the church after the sermon, apparently in distress. Duncan picked up his Bible to counsel her when his fellow worker, who had a keen sense of discernment, stopped him: 'Wait Duncan,' he whispered, 'I'll speak with her.'

He went to where she sat with her head in her hands, put his hand upon her shoulder and said: 'Get out of here, you child of the devil!'

With a startled scream she rose and fled from the church. Later it was revealed that she had been planted by the publican to feign conviction of sin in order to disturb the meeting and bring disrepute on God's servants.

In contrast, a beautiful incident also occurred during the same mission. Another young woman was attending nightly and was obviously interested. Her parents were antagonistic, and with social ambitions for their daughter, arranged for the son of a local laird to take her to a dance to distract her mind from the meetings.

As they danced, the young man talked disparagingly about the gospel and the Pilgrims. Pulling a tract from his pocket he began to laugh at the title—*Where is Hell? Hell is at the end of a Christless Life.* But his mockery had reached a climax and the girl, unable to endure it any longer, pushed him from her and ran from the hall, leaving her embarrassed partner in the middle of the floor.

Duncan was preaching when the church door opened. In stepped this beautiful girl, still in her evening dress and dancing slippers. She walked down the aisle, fell on her knees at the front of the church and said: 'Would someone please help me to find Jesus?'

A Christian periodical of 1921 carries an article with the arresting title: *Spiritual Awakening in Ardnamurchan*. Ardnamurchan, in Argyllshire, is the most westerly promontory of the mainland of Great Britain. The writer, a local farmer, told of scenes of revival such as he had not witnessed for the past twenty-five years. A convert, when asked if she would still attend dances replied: 'There will be no more dances: the promoters of these have been converted and are in the house of prayer.'

A visitor to one of these missions writes:

Up to 200 were packed into the schoolroom. They came to listen with interest and sincerity. Conviction of sin began to be felt and the cry, 'What must I do to be saved?' came from penitent souls. Boys and girls in their teens, as well as men and women, up to and over seventy years, were seeking the Saviour. Even people unable to attend the meetings were deeply concerned for their souls. When the mission closed a Prayer Union was formed, with an approximate membership of sixty.

Weekly Prayer Union meetings were organised to bring the converts together for fellowship and instruction in the Word of God. Returning to one of these groups for a series of meetings with the converts, Duncan asked an old friend: 'How are the lambs of the flock getting on?'

In his quaint way he replied: 'There's none lame yet!'

The Prayer Union strengthened the faith of the converts and their prayers and practical support were appreciated by the Pilgrims. One night two Prayer Union members met by the roadside; the older one was burdened. 'I feel the Pilgrims are in need and that we should take to them the £1 that is in the P.U. funds,' he said.

The Pilgrims were in a remote district with little support and when their benefactors arrived after tramping over the hills, they burst into shouts of praise. The cupboard was bare, and they had no money to buy food, but God who had promised to meet their needs had guided His servants to their door at the right moment.

Iona, where the first Christian missionaries to Scotland are reported to have arrived; Morven, famed for its everlasting hills; Ballachulish, with its slate-quarries and Episcopalian settlers; Kinlochleven, where the British Aluminium industry was pioneered; all were missioned

—not all with equal success, but none without some victory to record.

At the latter place, meetings were crowded from the commencement. A soul won at an open-air meeting was the first-fruit of a plentiful harvest. The power of God was manifest and between twenty and thirty professed faith in Christ in the hostel dining-room where the mission was held.

'If the Pilgrims are coming to Kinlochleven, they're not coming to *this* house,' declared two young sisters who were determined to avoid the preachers. However, an uncle who was a keen Christian caught one of them with guile and extracted a promise from her to attend a meeting. That night she was saved. Her sister scorned her at first, but withing a week she, too, was a follower of Jesus.

'What changed your attitude so suddenly?' one was asked.

'These men are different,' she replied, referring to other preachers she had heard. 'They are concerned for our souls, and that man speaking tonight transmitted his concern to me, and I had to do something about it.'

Behind each victory was a hard-fought battle. It wasn't all plain sailing. Sometimes the storms were literal: on the return trip from Iona the little ferry-boat ran into heavy seas. For two hours they rowed, Duncan helping the ferryman at the oars and arriving ashore with bleeding hands. At other times it was storms of criticism and abuse, often from the least expected sources, that left them with bleeding hearts.

After commencing a mission, in which God began to work, a local minister sent them a letter to the effect that they were disturbing the peace of the community and had

better leave. They committed the matter to God returning
a note to remind him that there is peace in a graveyard
but it is the peace of death! Happily, he got the message
and later apologised to the Pilgrims and became a willing
helper in the mission.

In the midst of opposition from whatever quarter, the
peace of God garrisoned their hearts. Duncan's favourite
fellow-Pilgrim, George Dunlop, often prayed: 'Lord
give us Thy peace that we may effectively serve Thee.'
This was the secret of steadfastness in the conflict.

Duncan acknowledged a great debt to George Dunlop
—'that dear Irish laddie, to whom I owe so much.' He
was deeply impressed by the quiet manner, disciplined
life and deep humility of his fellow worker. One night he
woke up to find him on his knees worshipping the Lord,
and was welcomed from slumberland with the salutation:
'Duncan, isn't the love of Jesus wonderful!'

Because of his knowledge of Gaelic Duncan took the
lead in visiting as some of the older people understood
little English. But George was not always left out. One
day they called with Donald Cameron as he worked on
his potato patch a few hundred yards from the Atlantic
Ocean. Donald spoke a few words in English, then he and
Duncan lapsed into Gaelic. 'I might as well have been
listening to Chinese,' George remarked.

Then Duncan asked: 'Will you pray, Donald?' The
big, brown-bearded man in simple, unhurried manner
lifted his voice to God in his native language and to
George every word became intelligible! He heard in his
own tongue, as on the day of Pentecost when they were
also with one accord in one place.

Each summer the Pilgrims led the annual open-air
campaign in Oban, a favourite holiday resort in the
Western Highlands. Night after night for two months

they told the story of saving grace to crowds sometimes reaching 500 in number.

One night a young man followed them to the hall where they were staying. He was in desperation: 'Can you help me? Strong drink is my master, but I believe Jesus can save me.' They pointed him to Christ and a few weeks later heard him relate publicly how his fetters were broken instantly when forgiveness, light and peace flooded his soul, and three of his relatives had since been saved.

Failte don Eilean Sgiathanach—Welcome to the Isle of Skye. A present day traveller crossing on the ferry to 'the Misty Isle' from Kyle of Lochalsh would be greeted with these words on a large banner. But when Duncan crossed over in 1924 to commence mission-work he was given the cold shoulder. Some unfortunate circumstance prior to his arrival had given the people a wrong impression of evangelistic work. Only a few faithful supporters, converts of previous missions, attended. Visiting produced no positive response, sometimes there was open antagonism. A woman slammed the door in his face, shouting: 'Clear out of the village. Clear out, you servants of the devil!'—an expression reckoned to be the worst insult you can throw at a religious person in the Highlands.

'Have faith in God,' is a motto of the Mission. Faith and prayer can remove mountains. One evening, faith to continue and confidently expect God to work was given when singing the hymn:

High are the cities that dare our assault;
  Strong are the barriers that call us to halt.
March we on fearless and down they must fall;
  Vanquished by faith in Him far above all.

Duncan gave himself to prayer, often walking the roads at night asking God to intervene. In the village were three young women who also knew how to pray. Leaving the meeting one night one of them said: 'God is going to work in this place; souls will be saved but we must fight the battle on our knees.'

They went home to pray. Duncan also prayed all night in a barn. After midnight one of the girls was assured that prayer would be answered and ran to the home of another with the message: 'God has come! God has come! He is going to work! But we must pray right through.' They continued until six in the morning.

Next night the power of God fell upon the meeting. Souls groaned under the convicting power of the Spirit of God. One woman left the meeting crying: 'I'm lost! I'm lost! There's no mercy for me!' She was brought back in and fell to the floor. No one could help her, until God revealed the saving power of His Son and brought peace to her troubled soul.

Attendance increased. The presence of God was felt through the entire community. Whole families were brought to Christ. A crofter, over seventy years old, became so active with the new life of Christ in him that people were amazed. His son, also saved then, tells how his father requested that he might sit at the communion table. 'And why do you want to come?' the minister inquired.

'I want something for my emptiness!' he replied, meaning he was hungry for more of Christ.

The old postman was a terrible drinker. No one thought of inviting him to the meetings. Probably he would not have gone if he had been invited. But one night his wife left for the church with her neighbours, and her husband, so peeved that he had been overlooked, thought: I'll go along just to spite them,' Off he went. God took hold of him and soon he was rejoicing in Christ.

Neilag was another of the 'wild 'uns' as far as drink was concerned. A petition was being organised to get the preacher out of the village and being one of the prominent men, a parish councillor, he went along armed with pencil and paper to write down objections and get fuel for warfare. But many had already come to scoff and stayed to be saved. God stepped in again. Neilag was converted.

He witnessed everywhere, speaking to everyone he met, even getting on his knees by the roadside to pray with them. Former friends thought he had lost his reason, but Neilag had lost his burden and could not help telling others. Questioned before going forward to the Lord's table, he told the ministers and elders that he went to Breakish expecting to find the devil with Duncan Campbell but found the Lord instead! 'That meeting was better than the chicken my wife had for tea!' he said.

Then one night one of the other converts arrived at the church terribly distressed. 'Oh, Mr. Campbell, Neilag's gone back! Neilag's gone back! I saw him going to the lodge with a bottle in his pocket.' Neilag had been invited by relatives to a dinner in honour of his grandmother's birthday and it was the custom for each guest to bring a bottle of whisky.

But Neilag returned later. A house-meeting was in progress and there he told his story. When he arrived at the lodge, his friends were delighted to see him, thinking he had turned his back on this wildfire religion, and to prove that they were not heathens they asked him to say the grace. He prayed for about twenty minutes, asking God to save them! Stunned, but still impenitent, they then asked him to propose the first toast to his grandmother. He took the bottle from his pocket, unwrapped it and poured the contents into the glasses, and, as he gleefully concluded: 'I made them drink the toast to my grandmother with the milk from the brown cow!'

Duncan was fearless in speaking the truth as he moved from village to village. Talking to a crofter one day he told him: 'Lachie, you're as hard as the devil can make you.' These plain words shook the big man who went to his room to pray and passed from death to life.

Other personal contacts also led to salvation. On his way home from a cottage meeting, he met three women walking by the shore. It occurred to him that they might be under conviction. 'Has God been dealing with you?' he asked.

'Yes, I'm anxious,' one replied, 'and I believe God has sent you to me.'

There among the rocks she knelt and yielded to Christ and then said: 'You must come and see my sister. She's also anxious and has been wanting to speak to you.' Her sister, too, entered the kingdom as the evening shadows fell across the distant Cuillins.

God worked in homes and on the hillside, as well as in the meetings. The Lord revealed Himself to a young girl as she was walking up the brae near her own home. The reality of God's love shown in the death of Christ so overwhelmed her that for a time she could hardly speak.

Even beyond the shores of the island relatives of those involved in the movement were saved: A young woman from one of the villages who was working on the mainland was moved to Christ, and a man on his way home from Australia was gripped with conviction of sin on the boat and converted before he reached the island.

A few nights after commencing one of his early missions on Skye, Duncan took suddenly ill and was confined to his lodgings. A medical examination showed suspected tuberculosis—a dreaded diagnosis fifty years ago.

Local Christians ministered faithfully to his needs, taking turns to watch at his bedside. They were naturally disappointed with this setback to their hopes and prayers, but accepted it with typical Scottish resignation as one of those adverse dispensations of Providence, not to be questioned.

But one young woman, among those responsible for organising the mission and who had prayed much for it, was not so easily diverted. Had God not promised to bless? Had He not pledged Himself to save souls? Would He now fail to keep His word? Of course not! He would honour His promise. Then, He must do something about it!

Her turn came to watch by the preacher's bedside. He looked as though he would never occupy a pulpit again; but with only a glance toward him she knelt to pray. Her prayer was simple and to the point: 'Lord, we invited him here, now it looks like we have him on our hands. But Lord, You are going to heal him and when You do, look after him, for the dear man hasn't the sense to look after himself!'

Outrageous? Presumptuous? Perhaps to a refined religious mind, concerned with liturgical niceties, it might sound so, but here it was the bold language of faith from a simple Highland lass, which was speedily rewarded.

From the moment she said 'Amen' a change came over the patient. His strength gradually returned and the following night he was back in the pulpit preaching with his old fiery zeal, urging sinners to seek the narrow way.

It was a glorious fight! What victories were won! But the heat of battle was beginning to have its effect again on the determined warrior. Suddenly, almost as abruptly as he left the battlefield in France, he was plucked from the spiritual conflict of missions—once more a casualty.

CHAPTER NINE

Upheavals and Heartburn

FROM Fort William, the 'gateway to the isles', the train daily winds its way through a succession of wild glens and along the margin of lochs which mirror the flanking hills on still April evenings.

But Duncan had little eye for the beauty on either side as it silently disappeared into the gathering mist. Several questions of a different nature occupied his mind. There was the immediate problem of his health and related to this, his future position in the Mission. He was unsettled also regarding his long-standing friendship and hopes of marriage.

Symptoms pointed to renewed lung infection with the possibility of admission to a sanatorium. A lady from Skye had consulted a radiologist known to her, and arranged an appointment in Glasgow. After thorough examination hospital treatment was not recommended, but he was told he had a strained heart, and was instructed to rest. He needed rest; he was not only physically ill, but at the point of nervous exhaustion.

With his Highland-loving wife, John George Govan followed the work of the Pilgrims in the north with interest. He was also concerned for the health of the workers,

and when it became clear that Duncan was no longer fit
for active mission-work he invited him to Edinburgh to
recuperate in the homely, spiritual atmosphere of the
Training Home.

The Govan family lived on the first floor, and this
home they now shared with their young friend. Duncan
never forgot the kindness of 'the Chief' and his wife.
He later named one of his sons in his memory.

The cook was instructed in the preparation of 'carra-
genn', a Highland health delicacy made from an edible
seaweed of that name, and very palatable to Highlanders!
But Mrs. Govan had greater difficulty in supervising a
diet for his tired mind. He was encouraged to read light,
easily digested literature, but with access to a library of
hefty theological volumes Duncan was keen to make good
use of them. When supposed to be resting Mrs. Govan
would find him sitting in the garden perusing Bunyan's
Sighs from Hell or Boston's *Fourfold State*. It was
useless trying to persuade him to surrender them. Instead
she asked the students to whisk them away unnoticed
when he laid them down.

During the day he busied himself with practical
household duties and was supposed to retire early, but
when he should have been asleep the students could hear
him praying fervently in Gaelic with Angus Robertson, a
brother from Skye.

Three months at the Training Home restored his
physical vitality but uncertainty about the future lingered.
The doctors had advised him to seek less strenuous
labour. What should he do? Was this sufficient guidance
on which to make a decisive move? Or should his original
call to Faith Mission work still have precedence over
fresh circumstances?

Some advised in one direction; some in another. In

his own mind a conflict of loyalties raged. There was no clear guidance and no peace.

Eleven years had passed since he had watched the blue-eyed lassie turn in the doorway of the barn to make her choice for Christ, and through the upheaval of the war and diverse paths he never wavered from the choice he had made that night. He waited, sometimes patiently, sometimes not so patiently, for the day when they would be together for life.

Shona was shy, but unconsciously drawn to him. He was confident. Her mother admired him and her brothers teased them, aided and abetted by his own parents. 'He spends more time in your house than in ours,' his mother said.

When he was in Skye, his father met Shona one day: 'When did you hear from Duncan?'

'He's coming on Thursday.'

'Oh well, we'll see him on Friday!'

She was in the Bible Training Institute in Glasgow when Duncan was demobilised in 1918 and later guided to work with Lilias Trotter of the Algiers Mission Band. Duncan proposed marriage then, but not wishing to go to the mission-field engaged, she declined and the chagrined suitor had to wait. Wondering if she would ever agree to marry him, he voiced his fears to her brother who merely remarked: 'I never met the girl yet who gave me heartburn!' Cold comfort for warm affection.

Two years later she returned and they met again at the Keswick Convention. She had been ill and confined to bed. It was only on the homeward train journey that they had opportunity to discuss the future. This was how he told the story of that journey some time later, when visiting South Africa. His hostess had cooked a big home-grown cabbage for dinner and was pleased to be entertaining the Convention speaker in her Johannesburg home but knew that he had to watch his diet.

'Do you like cabbage, Mr. Campbell?' she asked.

'Oh yes indeed . . . Now then, that is something I am particularly fond of.' The twinkle in his eye indicated that she had tapped an interesting story.

'Oh, how's that?'

'Well, I was at the Keswick Convention in 1924, ten years after falling in love with a certain young lady. We met again at the Convention and travelled home together. The train was crowded, and anxious to find a quiet spot where we could talk, we walked along the corridor until we came to the guard's van. He was an understanding gentleman; when we arrived, he went off! The only seats available were stacked bags of cabbages and there, among the cabbages I proposed to her, and she accepted. Do you wonder now that I have a weakness for cabbage?'

In July 1925 during a brief visit home Duncan wrote to Mr. Govan intimating his resignation from the Mission.

In December the same year the young couple were married in the Prince of Wales Halls in Glasgow. Their honeymoon holiday was spent on Skye, and in the village of Dunvegan, with its picturesque castle and famous fairy flag, the door opened to a new sphere of service.

Until then, Duncan had been working on the farm, awaiting the next step. In Dunvegan he was asked to preach in the United Free Church and this was followed by an invitation to remain on Skye as a missionary.

To the south of the island in 'the garden of Skye' is the remote, sleepy, little village of Ardvasar. The church by the roadside was vacant and the Presbytery asked Duncan to take charge of it. Opposite the church stood a well-appointed manse to which he brought his bride.

The people of Ardvasar at that time may have been content to let the world go by, but it could not be said that they were indifferent to church affairs. There was strong religious feeling in the community, not always of a charitable kind. Three denominations—the Church of Scotland, the Free Church and the United Free Church—advocated their brands of Presbyterianism within the bounds of the small parish. When the minister of one church visited families from his congregation in the outlying district of Camus Cross, he passed a small cottage on the way. The woman who lived there, a member of one of the other churches, eventually complained that he did not call with her.

'Well,' answered the cleric warily, 'It's at Camus Cross I have my sheep.'

'Aye, and your goats too,' was the indignant retort!

It is said that Highlanders are a sentimental and emotional type of people who enjoy seasons of devotion at communions and missions, but lack practical outreach in their Christianity. (That is the opinion of a Highlander with more heather than most in his garden!) But it could never be said that the new missionary in Ardvasar was impractical. The older people in the village remember him as a vehement and forthright preacher and a conscientious visitor. He cycled miles, often late at night, to be at the bedside of the sick and at harvest time was in the fields helping the crofters, especially the old folk and widows.

Everyone was visited irrespective of denomination, and where possible good relationships were cultivated with other churches, especially at communion services. Many were quickened to new spiritual heights and some added to the church as Duncan preached.

But meanwhile a storm was brewing which forced a

dilemma upon the young missionary, and produced a
setback in church relations. Ironically, it was an effort to
unite two of the churches that caused the upheaval.
Negotiations had opened between the United Free
Church Assembly and the General Assembly of the
Church of Scotland with a view to sinking past differences
and bringing the two bodies together.

A minority, headed by the Rev. James Barr, objected
to the proposal. Barr opposed the Establishment Principle
and was also afraid that the Union would result in a
return to the system of patronage which led to the famous
Disruption in 1843. The Establishment Principle was the
support of the church by State endowments rather than
by voluntary contributions. Patronage was the appointment of ministers without the consent of the people. Mr.
Barr and his followers determined to safeguard their
freedom to speak out against the state where necessary
in the spirit of the Covenanters and Reformers. There
were undoubted advantages in State connections, such as
financial assistance and obligatory facilities for worship
in isolated communities, but for them the dangers out-
weighed the advantages. State support could eventually
curtail freedom of speech.

Duncan sided with the minority which opted not to
join with the Church of Scotland, and remained as the
United Free Church Continuing when the Act of Union
was signed in 1929. It has been alleged that his motive for
doing so was a secret hope of early ordination within the
continuing body, but available facts demonstrate that he
would have been better off in every way had he supported
the Union.

Not particularly concerned about the issues of patronage and endowments, Duncan believed that the evangelical message and the temperance movement, which he

supported ardently, would have more freedom and thrust, cut loose from the ties of a state mooring.

The Presbyteries of Skye, however, were overwhelmingly in favour of the Union, and while many of his congregation shared the views of their dissenting missionary, they were powerless to form a branch of the continuing church. Consequently, Duncan resigned his charge.

It was no light step. The added responsibility of three children left no room for indulging in a display of ecclesiastical adventuring. Only his concern to have a clear conscience caused him to act contrary to the counsel of his colleagues. Duncan had no desire to offend anyone, but would never sacrifice principle for popularity. He wrote: 'We are not to be men pleasers; we live unto God. We do not take our instructions from others; it is not to them we render our account.' His decision was not popular as the following story indicates.

Travelling from Edinburgh by train a few months later, three ministers from northern congregations, returning from the General Assembly, occupied a compartment with him. He was unknown to them, and taking him for a lowland farmer, they nodded a brief greeting and then began to discuss the affairs of the church in Gaelic, unaware that their quiet companion understood every word.

Soon the tide of conversation reached the shores of Ardvasar and its waves lapped around the doings and influence of the former missionary. Two of them denounced him as a troublemaker; the other countered: 'Well, if I was as young as he is, and had my ministry to begin again, I would do the same thing. I think he is to be admired for his courage.'

The train reached Inverness. Luggage was unloaded amid greetings and farewells, and the three ministers were taking leave of each other, when the 'farmer' approached them. Gripping the hand of the one who had defended him, he said in perfect Gaelic: 'Thank you for speaking for me when talking about Ardvasar.' The other two suddenly disappeared!

Upheavals similar to the one in Ardvasar occurred throughout the country. Many groups of believers had no desire to be absorbed in the machinery of the State Church and fought to retain their independence.

In Balintore, a small salmon-fishing village neatly tucked away behind the hills and loans of Fearn on the north-east coast, the battle raged. Here the entire community voted unanimously to break their association with the neighbouring church of Nigg and remain out of the Union. The United Free Church of Balintore was formed. In March 1930 Duncan was appointed to shepherd the new flock and formally ordained as a missionary in the church with authority to dispense the sacraments.

CHAPTER TEN

On the Pastoral Front

THE people of Balintore were excited about their new church. The recent breach had aroused interest; people who never attended church before now came regularly. The young people enjoyed the dispute and found a spice of adventure in belonging to an independent group. When the new minister arrived enthusiasm increased.

Duncan's first sermon settled his popularity in Balintore. There was a hushed silence as the congregation dispersed but the village soon buzzed with excitement. 'What a man this is!' exclaimed one old fellow. 'Did you hear him on Paul today?'

'Man, but he's an apostle Paul himself!' another replied.

The new minister did not try to be popular. He was too straightforward and uncompromising for that. His words hit hard. Older unconverted people were told they were 'gathering speed for hell', and he warned the younger ones to place no hope in the ghost of future repentance. 'Be careful,' he said 'lest God should refuse the devil's leavings.' Honest! Truthful! Passionate! That was how these God-fearing fisher-folk liked their religion, and that was how their new pastor preached it.

Practical difficulties had to be overcome. The new congregation had no church building. Services were held in a dilapidated hall known as 'the meeting-house'. This dingy little place was too small, and often the communion services were held under the open sky in a nearby field.

Depending mainly on the harvest of the sea for a livelihood, the people of Balintore were not wealthy at the best of times, and during the early Thirties the gloom of economic depression hung over the entire country. Money was scarce, but they were determined to have their own building. Fellowship was as necessary as food. The old school at Hilton was used for worship while the meeting-house was demolished and the stones cleaned to rebuild on the same site. Through hard work and sacrificial giving a new church was opened on the 7th December, 1932. A manse also was erected beside the church.

Eight years before Duncan Campbell arrived in Balintore revival had swept through the village when two Faith Mission Pilgrims were preaching in the district. The members of the church were mainly converts of this movement and gave strong, vigorous prayer support to their pastor.

He was loved by everyone, old and young alike. His native language contributed to his acceptance with the older people. Gaelic and grace have sometimes been married in the thinking of Highlanders, as in the mind of an old woman who, hearing of the death of a non-Gaelic speaker, expressed deep sorrow that he had gone to meet his Maker without the Gaelic! In 1930 Gaelic was no longer being spoken by the young people on the northeast coast, and a young man who could converse and preach in it must be indeed very spiritual !

Duncan Campbell was not a trained theologian. When Marconi was quizzed about the technical details of his wireless telegraphy he simply looked at the equipment and said: 'It works.' Duncan had the same attitude to theology. He did not stop to get involved in time-consuming arguments. Even 'born-again Barbie', the local 'theologian', couldn't correct his views on election! He knew God could save and transform lives. He had seen it happen. It worked. That was enough. He was a practical theologian. All his life he sought to put into practice what he believed. If a man's Christianity didn't work out, it wasn't worth having, no matter how correct its logic, or how orthodox its theology.

He could be unorthodox in the pulpit. Sometimes the order of service would go by the board. He would scrap his notes, tell the congregation: 'The Holy Spirit has taken charge of this meeting,' and then pray—prayer was wrung from him at such times. Then the elders would pray until the presence of God filled the church. A lady remembers the presence of Jesus being so real beside her on one of these occasions, that she instinctively drew back from where she was sitting, feeling unfit to be so near to the holiness of the Lord.

At the evening service one Sunday a psalm was being sung before the sermon when suddenly Duncan felt he could not give his prepared message, and as the strains of the last verse died away, a text from Isaiah came into his mind. He had never preached on it before, but its message unfolded to him as he spoke, and there was evidence that God worked in lives that night. He later returned to the same text hoping to preach on it again, but was unable to prepare a sermon, or even remember anything he had said that evening.

He used the same sermons repeatedly and didn't always

write them down—but someone else did! A young woman who worked as a receptionist for the doctor often had to attend to telephone calls on Sunday afternoon. Only recently converted, she was hungry for the Word of God, and, while waiting for calls, exercised her mind by recalling the sermon she had heard that morning and putting it on paper.

One day an elder came to Duncan and said: 'That was a good sermon you preached. I read it this morning.'

'You couldn't have! I didn't write it down.'

'No, no, but Kitty did.'

A while later Duncan burst into Kitty's home: 'Where's my sermon?'

'What sermon?' she asked.

'The one you wrote down. I'm going over to Nairn to preach and I want to use it again!' Constant repetition never weakened the power of the truth he proclaimed.

Lighter moments were enjoyed with the fishermen too. He wanted to go out on the boats but they were reluctant to take him as some of them thought it was unlucky to have a minister on board. One morning he went down to the harbour determined to put to sea. Unable to dissuade him, one eventually said: 'Well, Mr. Campbell, if you're coming with us you'd better go and get your coat. It'll be cold out there.' Up to the manse he hurried, thinking he had defeated their superstition at last, but when he came back they were gone!

They teased him about striking the pulpit with his fist. Even the children imitated his style on the school desks. Later, when he broke a bone in his wrist at this exercise, someone asked: 'But what about the pulpit?'

These suffered too! When a new one was needed in Balintore someone insisted: 'Oh, surely this one will do.'

'But it's cracked,' said Duncan.

'Well, it was yourself that cracked it!' remarked a woman who was listening.

He visited each home regularly without any pre-arranged protocol, just 'dropping in' unexpectedly. Opening the door he usually announced his presence by shouting down the hallway: 'Is there anybody in?' and when a response was heard he quickly added: 'Is that the kettle I hear singing?' Over a cup of strong tea he would discuss the weather and local news, then quickly and naturally turn the conversation to spiritual matters. He spent no more time in any place than was necessary but never concluded a visit without prayer.

In addition to the usual church services he had many preaching engagements in other districts as well as open-air meetings in the village, and to the delight of the older residents who were too feeble to attend church he conducted Gaelic services in their homes. He aimed to reach everyone and welcomed any evangelists who came to the district. In 1939 three Pilgrims set off in an old fourteen-seater bus to undertake a seven-hundred-mile evangelistic tour of the north of Scotland. Near Balintore the bus broke down and Duncan, hearing of their plight, arrived on the scene. Soon the minister, with his jacket off and shirt-sleeves rolled up, was underneath the vehicle doing what he could to effect a repair; and until a spare part was posted on he entertained the stranded travellers in the manse.

Duncan's chief work in Balintore was among the young people. He had a great influence over them, particularly the early teenagers. His style of preaching appealed. They liked his robust, unconventional manner and down-to-earth talks. He cared for them and would go to any lengths to help them. As he preached and prayed many committed their lives to Jesus Christ.

A Christian Endeavour meeting was formed and here Duncan, and Mrs. Campbell, encouraged the young people to follow the Lord. 'It is in youth that character is formed which is the determining factor right through life,' he told them.

A grocer in Bonar Bridge gave him an old car. When preaching elsewhere he would fill it with the young people, who went along to sing and testify. It was a temperamental vehicle, and one night, returning from Strathpeffer Convention, it chugged to a halt on a lonely stretch of road by Invergordon Bay. When trying, without much success, to locate the fault in the darkness, the searchlight from a minesweeper in the bay lit up the road a short distance in front. Duncan immediately instructed the young people to push the car into the light. The captain on the ship seeing what had happened kept the light on them till the trouble was corrected and they could proceed. Next Sunday Duncan used the incident to instruct his listeners to place themselves under the light of God's Word where sin can be located and the remedy applied.

The young people, following his example, were full of zeal in speaking to others about the Saviour. One, a girl called Kate, was filled with the Spirit during a time of prayer in the manse. The joy of the Lord shone in her face. Everyone noticed it. 'She can't come in to buy a twopenny stamp without speaking about Christ,' a shopkeeper said. Kate's witness brought many to Christ, and she had hoped to go into mission-work after completing her nursing training, but took ill and returned home to die. She was only twenty-one when the Saviour came for her and leaving her widowed mother by the bedside she went to be with Him.

Kate's triumphant death and Duncan's spiritual guidance moved the other young folk to a closer walk with God, and unknown to them was preparing many more for an early entry into the presence of the Lord. One was drowned shortly after; another died from tuberculosis, and nine were killed on active service. Five died on Sunday, 15th October, 1939, when the battleship *Royal Oak* was torpedoed during a daring raid by a German U-boat in Scapa Flow, a natural harbour in the Orkney Islands. With a heavy heart Duncan walked around the village that evening to break the news to relatives and friends. The following Sunday at a memorial service he preached from Jeremiah on *The Sorrow of the Sea*, reminding them that Christians are not immune from sorrow, but in their affliction they have the companionship of a Saviour and Comforter who 'retains our tears in His bottle, but eternally hides our sin'.

Five months later it was a further blow to hear that he had accepted a call to the United Free Church in Falkirk. They were reluctant to let him go. He had shared their joys and sorrows, and with so many of their young men gone to the war they felt they needed him. But his ministry in Balintore was finished. There were no special farewell sermons on his last Sunday with them, just the old gospel he had preached so often, pleading with those yet unsaved to respond to the claims of Christ: 'Will all these years be in vain, the talks, the fellowship, the warnings, the entreaties? Oh, sinner, come! Yet there is room.'

Ten fruitful years had been spent in their midst. Church membership had steadily increased. Many owed their Christian experience to his faithful work. His own family had increased to three boys and two girls, and when they all left for a new way of life in the industrial south the entire congregation gathered at Fearn station to say farewell.

It is customary in the United Free Church for an ordained missionary who has proved himself in his preaching and polity to be promoted to the status of a minister after some years of service. The Church recognised the excellent work Duncan had done in establishing the new church in Balintore and two years after moving to Falkirk he received this honour. Speaking at the General Assembly, he fearlessly challenged the Church to fulfil her primary calling. Like Thomas Chalmers, he believed that a church is not an end in itself, but a means to promote the Christian good of the population. When through restraints from whatever quarter, it becomes incapable of contributing, as it should, to the promotion of evangelical religion and ceases to be a soul-saving agency, it has lost the very reason for its existence.

Duncan's new parish was the scene of industrial expansion and a much tougher battleground than Balintore. Material prosperity often breeds spiritual indifference. He sowed the same seed and preached with the same fervour, but there was not the same response. Even a large united mission to the town conducted by Dr. Alan Redpath failed to produce the results he had hoped for in his own congregation.

The lack of spiritual growth and concern among many who professed Christ was a sore trial to him. His vigorous Highland nature required vision and experiences to inspire him. He moved between the mountain-top and the valley and could not endure the dead flat atmosphere of spiritual sterility. 'When you work with the iron, the iron gets into your soul,' he complained. Nevertheless he stuck to the path of duty, worked hard, and his labour was not wholly unrewarded for there were several victories in the battle for souls.

One of these almost involved him in a literal fight! A

formerly godless woman had been converted and wished to have her family baptised. Duncan went to the home where the children were lined up to be sprinkled. One wee fellow didn't like it; when his turn came he put his fists up and said: 'You'll put no water on me, mister!'

Duncan's programme was always full—hours of study and prayer before breakfast; miles of cycling to visit his people in Falkirk and the neighbouring towns of Grangemouth, Larbert and Camelon; three services, plus the open-air, each Sunday; a monthly Gaelic Service, and other preaching engagements throughout Scotland and in Ireland—he was a busy man.

He worked in close co-operation with other Christian leaders in the town and once a week met with some for prayer at six o'clock in the morning. Frequently he exchanged pulpits and assisted others in their activities. When Dr. Tom Fitch came to Bainsford Church of Scotland for a special mission, Duncan gave his support by cancelling his own week-night engagements. God extended His kingdom on that occasion, and Duncan's comment was: 'Who but the Holy Spirit could have accomplished so much with only the distribution of a few advertising leaflets and the prayers of God's people.' Dr. Fitch said that he never showed any spirit of envy at the outward spiritual success of others, but rejoiced in a pure, unsullied way, although he must have longed for similar blessing in his own congregation.

He conducted a baptismal service in the same church when the minister was ill. In the congregation was a young ex-Army lieutenant who was studying at an Agricultural College in Edinburgh. He had been drinking heavily, making life miserable for his mother, and was now in church for the second time since the age of twelve. His agnostic beliefs had recently been shaken by a

Bible verse on the advertising panel of a bus, and he now
tells how they received their death-blow that Sunday in
church:

> When Duncan Campbell came down from the pulpit
> to perform the baptism there was a light shining in his
> face so that I could hardly look at him. He then preach-
> ed about Paul and the fear of God shook me. I met him
> later in the manse, where he counselled me and read
> the story of the prodigal son. I had heard it before, but
> was surprised to learn that it was in the Bible! As he
> talked about the Christian life and the way of salvation
> I produced a packet of cigarettes and offered him one.
> He refused, so I lit one myself but before he was finished
> speaking I had decided to stop drinking and smoking,
> and threw the remainder of the cigarettes into the fire.
> I was very proud and he knew it. 'Are you willing
> to be a fool for Christ's sake?' he asked. 'Yes,' I
> replied. So we knelt to pray, and as he prayed a great
> change came over me, clear and unmistakable—Jesus
> Christ had come into my life! I got down on my knees
> one man, and rose up another.
> Then he asked me to support the open-air meeting
> at Callender Riggs and I was struck with terror. But I
> went along and stood next to the minister—that would
> appear respectable at any rate! What followed was
> worse. He asked me to speak. Wishing the ground
> would open up to receive me, I stepped forward. I
> have no idea what I said, but a great blessing flooded
> my soul as I witnessed for Christ. Next Sunday I even
> carried the portable organ up the High Street—a fool
> for Christ's sake!

CHAPTER ELEVEN

A New Beginning

To outward observers Duncan at this stage was a diligent, faithful pastor but inwardly there was dissatisfaction. He had lost something. God was still using him but there was not the conscious communion with God that he had once enjoyed.

The impressions of his battlefield experience had receded, and the vision of Christ was no longer a reality. No longer did he 'feel as pure as an angel'; the corruption and deceitfulness of his heart were pre-eminent again. He was proud of the fact that he had been invited to speak at five conventions in one year; proud that he had been used in revival: but now frustration, failure and defeat stared him in the face. He realised he was clinging to the decaying threads of past experiences and striving vainly to maintain a reputation built upon them.

When Duncan first entered the ministry, liberal ideas were being taught with an aura of respectability. For a short while he came under the influence of these, picking up seeds of doubt regarding Biblical inspiration and authority. His doubts were short-lived and never openly expressed, but nevertheless they helped to quench some of the conviction and power in his preaching.

But lying further back on the road to relapse was the ever-present doubt as to whether or not he had taken the right step in resigning from the Faith Mission. There appeared to be some connection between his decision to leave the Mission and his spiritual condition. It is significant that with the awareness of barrenness and spiritual defeat came a strong conviction that he should return to mission-work.

Over a period of four years he felt that the Lord might be leading him back. His gifts lay more in the direction of evangelistic work than pastoral ministry and his personal interests were also slanted this way. An invitation to lecture at the Mission's Training Home and Bible College in Edinburgh seemed to confirm this inclination, and it received further impetus when someone from within the Mission asked him if he had ever thought of returning.

Various other openings were presented but failed to appeal: there was mention of a Church of Scotland appointment as a Gaelic evangelist to the Highlands, also he was due to preach in Arbroath with a view to accepting a vacant charge there. With negotiations in hand for three possible appointments he was, to put it mildly, confused and uncertain.

At the same time he was asking himself some honest questions about his spiritual life, and the belief was growing upon him that if he was to know any peace and satisfaction again in Christian service it would be in the ranks of the Mission. When the children were asleep and Mrs. Campbell was sitting darning she could hear him praying in his room: 'O Lord, tell me what I should do.' He discussed the situation in detail with his wife, and with a friend as they walked together in the countryside, seeking to become aware of the implications for everyone concerned. But the matter had to be resolved between himself and the Master. It involved more than a change of location; spiritual readjustment was necessary. Gradually his spirit of discontent increased until a crisis was reached.

Early one morning he was busy as usual in the study when he was suddenly confronted with what he described as his 'years of backsliding... a barren, spiritual wilderness'. He felt small. Here he was busy in the Saviour's work, but a stranger to His intimate presence. He recalled days when it had been a delight to spend time in His company. Also, the days, when as a Pilgrim in the Faith Mission he had seen times of spiritual awakening in Argyllshire, were brought to his mind in vivid contrast with his present ministry. Then came the question which shattered him: 'When did you last lead a soul to Jesus?'

At that time he was preparing to address the Edinburgh 'Keswick' Convention. The other speaker at the Convention was Dr. Tom Fitch. At one of the services, Dr. Fitch related some of his own personal experiences which intensified Duncan's sense of need. Feeling unfit to be on the platform, he cried to God where he sat: 'Oh Lord, give me back the years that the locusts have eaten. Make again the marred vessel.'

It was late when he arrived home. Supper was ready but he refused to eat, and went straight to his study. On his face in front of the fire he battled with the powers of darkness. Had God cast him off? The devil whispered that God had no further use for him, but into the womb of despair came a seed of hope and faith when a verse from the Psalms took hold of his mind: 'For the Lord will not cast off his people, neither will He forsake His inheritance.' This was followed by another word from Psalm 103: 'Who forgiveth all thine iniquities; who healeth all thy diseases.' Instantly a new consciousness of the love of God swept over him like waves of the sea until he wondered if he could endure it any longer. The inner cleansing he had experienced when a wounded soldier was a reality once more, bringing healing to his spirit.

The joy of forgiveness and release was deep, but faded again when he realised that God was indeed calling him to return to the work of evangelism. There was still an unwillingness in his heart, perhaps because it would cost others more than it would cost him. What about the children in the midst of their education? Would that be completed. With Mrs. Campbell, he was concerned to motivate each member of the family to higher education and worthwhile jobs. Also it would involve long periods away from home, giving added family responsibilities to Mrs. Campbell, and he would not have the same guaranteed salary. How could he ask others to share the sacrifice he must make?

As these thoughts passed through his mind the meaning of the cross became clear: 'He that loveth father or mother more than me is not worthy of me; and he that loveth son or daughter more than me is not worthy of me. And he that taketh not his cross, and followeth after me, is not worthy of me' (Matt. 10:37-38). His obedience to God would affect others also. This was inescapable, but whatever the cost he must obey; it would cost infinitely more not to obey.

Immediately he seemed to be in a trance gazing into caverns of death, witnessing the agonies of hell. With horror he saw thousands from the Highlands and Islands of Scotland drifting to their doom, and heard a voice calling: 'Go to them, go to them.'

Duncan always believed in the existence of hell but from that moment it was an unquestioning reality. Lost souls were really lost. He must warn them. He must tell them of God's way of escape. No longer could he think of personal sacrifice when souls were in danger. As he yielded to the way of the cross, peace stole over his heart again, assuring him that God would fit him to take up the ministry he had left years before.

Next morning he told his wife of his decision and then wrote three letters: one to the Session Clerk, another to the Presbytery Convener and the third to the Clerk of Assembly intimating that he was resigning from his charge, but wished to remain a member of the Presbytery and Denomination, retaining his status as a minister.

It was a step of faith to accept the call of God and return to the Faith Mission after twenty-three years in a settled ministry, but it would also be a step of faith for the Mission to re-accept someone of his age, for he was now fifty years old, and the Mission concentrated mainly on harnessing the energies of youth, engaging in a type of itinerant evangelism better suited to unmarried workers.

The Council were cautious when Duncan inquired about returning. They were reluctant to accept responsibility for a married man with a family; some regarded the idea as a departure from its original practice and and procedure. Then there was the question of accommodation. The only house available was a cottage in Glenelg, a small Highland village in Inverness-shire, but living in this isolated community would make it difficult for the children to continue at High School and University.

It gradually became clear to the Council that his application was in God's plan and in October 1948 he was offered an appointment to engage in evangelism in the Highlands, commencing on January 1st, 1949. Special prayer for the removal of all obstacles was answered.

The receipt of a substantial legacy at the Mission's Headquarters in Edinburgh made possible the purchase of a house in the city as a home for him and his family.

The problems of this period were like some jig-saw puzzle which seemed impossible to resolve. But behind the human involvements God was fitting the pieces together at both ends, preparing Duncan spiritually and psychologically for the difficult change, and also preparing the Mission for a new venture of faith.

The result was soon evident. The extent to which Duncan was moved in his night of encounter with God was felt immediately in his preaching and praying. The old despondency and defeat were gone, a new fighting spirit entered into him. The awareness of God with him was obvious in family worship as well as in public ministry. The matter of his re-entry into the Mission finally settled, he was happy and relaxed, and his soul soared to heights of spiritual communion and power which had been a mocking memory for years. The recurring theme in his preaching was 'the recovering grace of God'. 'How glad I am,' he repeated, 'that God is a God of new beginnings,' and then he would go on to illustrate his experience with the story of the prisoner who, filled with despair on hearing the poem about a bird with a broken pinion that never soared so high again, met the Saviour, and wrote another verse:

> But the soul that comes to Jesus,
> Through failure, shame and pain;
> By His wondrous love and mercy,
> May soar as high again.

When it became known that Duncan was released to conduct missions, invitations began to pour into Headquarters. These included a request from the Island of Skye. It is not surprising that his first preference was to return to the scene of former battles and resume the fight where he had left off nearly a quarter-of-a-century before.

CHAPTER TWELVE

An Old Battleground

THE young fellow clamped down the telephone receiver and leaned back in the chair. He was shaking, and the puzzled frown on his features deepened to a look of alarm.

'What on earth's going on up there?' he muttered. 'Have they taken leave of their senses? They must all be mad!'

He worked in an uncle's business in Glasgow and had just been on the phone to his home in Skye. The conversation had centred around a man called Campbell who was conducting a mission there, and strange things were happening. His brother had been 'converted', they said, and now it was his cousin. His cousin! A favourite boozing pal! Not he of all people! He thought of the 'good times' they had had together 'bending weel to the bottle' in like-minded company.

'How could he be influenced with this religious nonsense,' he mused. 'He has more sense than that.' Desperately he tried to shake off the disturbing emotions that crept over him and make himself believe it was not real. But he could not wish away hard facts; the questions kept coming. 'What if it is true? Well, if it is, something extraordinary must be taking place! In any case what business is it of mine? I don't need to get involved.'

But he felt involved, and against his will was drawn to the events that were taking place on the island. 'I know what I'll do,' he decided, 'I'll take the weekend off and see for myself what's happening. Maybe I'll be able to talk sense into them.'

With a ·22 rifle in the boot he headed north, and on the way stopped to shoot a stag; it would be nice to have venison for his friends! But a short distance from where he cut up the carcass a puncture stopped him, and to his dismay a gamekeeper and his dog appeared as he was changing the wheel. The boot-lid went down fast. The gamekeeper offered assistance, which he could not easily refuse, while all the time the dog sniffed excitedly at the rear, bringing more perspiration to the poacher's forehead than changing a wheel required! The job done, he produced a bottle of whisky and gave his helper a dram, hoping it would drown any curiosity as to why he put the flat tyre and the tools on the back seat instead of into the boot!

It was late when he reached Skye and he didn't expect to be introduced so quickly to the religious excitement, but a house-meeting was just ending at his brother's home when he walked in.

From the seclusion of the scullery he listened to the singing. It was a Scottish paraphrase, warning those who refused to listen to the Word of God, that they would one day be filled with the bitter fruits of sin, when it would be too late to pray. It scared him, and there was something unusual about the atmosphere in the home, which added to his discomfort. It seemed so solemn, or something—he couldn't describe it, but decided: 'This is no place for me. I'm getting back to Glasgow as soon as I can!'

The following day he was tinkering with the car at his parents' home when a minister entered the drive. 'Oh bother, this must be the notorious Duncan Campbell!' Not wishing to speak to him, he quickly found something under the bonnet needing attention.

The crunch of feet on the gravel path came nearer, then stopped. There was a light tap on his shoulder, and he emerged from the bowels of the car to receive an energetic handshake and a friendly greeting: 'Well, well, well, you must be the boy from Glasgow. I'm very pleased to see you.' And before he could reply the minister continued: 'You know, I have a promise from God that one day you will be a minister, preaching the gospel with me!'

What a prospect! Shaken and dumbfounded for a moment, his reaction soon changed to one of annoyance and suspicion. Concluding that the man was trying to hypnotise him—a rumour that had been circulated on the island—he brushed him off. 'You'd better go in and tell that to my father and mother. They might believe your fairy tales.'

Unperturbed by this attitude Duncan continued to chat and the young fellow was impressed with his kind and courteous manner. Duncan was sure that God had spoken to him, and had not a Christian woman in the village in a dream seen this same young man walking down the path to her house wearing a minister's collar?

That night, he consented to drive his aged father to church, intending to return home immediately but the old man prevailed upon him to wait for the service. He met his cousin and finding his attitude and conversation completely changed, concluded that he was ill! But listening to the preacher he began to feel that God was in the church, speaking to him and saw that *he* was the sick man, but was unwilling to admit it. 'Once out of here,' he thought, 'I'll put plenty of distance between myself and this man Campbell, or I'll be caught in the net too!'

Next morning he returned to Glasgow and plunged deeper into sin, trying to banish from his mind the events of the weekend, but it was going to be more difficult to put distance between himself and God than to run away from God's servant.

Meantime, the villages of Skye continued to be stirred. One minister said that he had witnessed nothing like it for over twenty years. But victory had not been gained easily. Former converts and other leading Christians were anxious to see many turning to Christ, but others were equally anxious to hinder the work, raising active opposition, reminiscent of Duncan's earlier missions on the island, when a local minister had to climb through a window to open the school for a service after the schoolmaster had locked them out! This time a doctor supported the rumour that he was hypnotising the people, influencing many away from the missions. Another man did much harm with a well-hatched scheme. Duncan was asked to visit him and found the man and his wife sitting by the fireside with solemn looks and distressed appearance. When he began to speak to them about the Saviour, the woman fell on her knees and began to weep, but they were crocodile tears. Her husband jumped up, ordered Duncan out, following him to the door with a well-aimed kick 'that would have startled a horse'. 'I saw you playing your eyes on her!' he shouted. 'You hypnotised her!'

This rumour was rife throughout the island, lowering attendance at the services in several places, but a minister wisely advised: 'Remain quiet, and God will overrule.'

God turned the tide unexpectedly through the conversion
of a respected young man. When asked to use his influence against the mission he replied: 'You know the
trouble that overtook my father twenty-five years ago
because of drunkenness. If this man Campbell hypnotises
people then he must have hypnotised my father the last
time he was here. He never touched drink since, and has
been for years an office-bearer in the church. No, I will
have nothing to do with it until I hear him myself.'

He began to attend and one night lingered behind to
buy a Gaelic Bible. 'You need more than a Gaelic Bible,'
Duncan told him, 'you need the mercy of God.' The following night he professed faith in Christ. The community
was deeply impressed and the confidence of the people
restored.

Duncan wrote: 'I am again fighting the old battle I
fought twenty-five years ago, but enjoying it on the
victory side.' Conviction of sin was deep but when the
light of the gospel broke upon the penitent the resulting
change was all the more glorious. A farmer was so
overjoyed by the sense of deliverance he received, that he
stood up and publicly declared that his burden was gone—
a remarkable action for a reserved Skyeman! A man who
was associated with the drink trade faced a reduced income
after his conversion, but his wife was heard to say: 'It's
better to be poor and have Christ than to be rich without
God. We have made our choice.'

House-meetings were requested by the converts to
which they invited their friends, and homes became
trysting places with God. Duncan pursued his old policy
of extensive visitation in each district regardless of the
weather. One landlady scolded him for going out in a
storm: 'Do you think the Lord intends you to go out in
weather like that?' He just smiled and carried on,

blissfully unaware of how incongruous he looked in her husband's sea-boots and his own clerical collar. When he was visiting, the people with Highland deference to a minister would stop work and gather in the house while he 'conducted worship'. This took the form of a little service and sometimes he ministered at as many as seven of these in one day.

Some districts were more affected than others. In one village every home was represented at the meetings. When the monthly film show came to the school not one person turned up; all the young people were at the mission.

In the Highlands Duncan made none of the usual evangelistic appeals. Reared on a diet of oatmeal porridge and the Shorter Catechism, Highland folk are blessed with the caution of a Calvinistic conscience, and regard such methods as 'man-made innovations' in the work of God. But in order that converts might be encouraged publicly to declare their acceptance of Christ when it was evident that God was at work, he announced short prayer-meetings, or after-meetings, to which the Christians were invited and also any who desired to follow Christ. He counselled individuals who sought help after the services, but preferred to hear of men and women having transactions with God without any human involvement.

In the course of visitation he was often led to anxious seekers and to those with spiritual difficulties whom he could help from the Word. A recurring problem in the religious experience of Highland people is a desire for manifestations, such as dreams and visions, before they will believe that the invitation of the gospel is for them. After all, it might be presumptuous to seek God without some evidence of being one of the elect! Consequently there is a prevailing lack of assurance. When Duncan was counselling those who had heard the voice of God and were faced with this mental block, he repeatedly turned to John 10:27 emphasising that it is God's sheep who hear His voice and may receive eternal life by faith. It was at this point that the light of the gospel shone into many hearts and minds with peace and assurance.

Duncan was often asked why there were more physical and supernatural manifestations in Christian work in the Highlands than elsewhere. This problem of assurance, he suggested, was the main reason. God in His goodness granted these manifestations to encourage weak and trembling faith to grasp the promises of life.

There were frequent prostrations, but these were noticeably confined to particular areas where people looked for them. Some endured unnecessary distress by unconsciously seeking a particular manifestation rather than God Himself, as in the case of a man who kept praying that God would give him the same experience as his neighbour had when he was saved. Duncan advised him to receive Christ and be satisfied with whatever degree of emotion God chose to give him. He warned: 'What conviction do you require to receive Christ? Only what makes you conscious that you are a sinner. God knows what you are able to bear. Perhaps if He answered your prayer and gave you the same experience as Donald, it could topple your reason.'

'I'm surprised at a man of your experience giving me advice like that Mr. Campbell!' was the indignant reply.

The man continued to pray as before. God answered his prayer and the next time Duncan saw him he was between two warders being taken to a mental hospital. They met after he was discharged, and all he could say was: 'Mr. Campbell, I'm a wiser man today.' Until his death, almost twenty years later, he lived consistently for Christ.

Duncan did not encourage physical manifestations, but was careful not to despise what God saw fit to permit. He recognised that they were a feature of revivals in the past, though not always helpful, sometimes raising opposition.

When rumour and obloquy failed to halt the forward march of God's purposes the devil made other attempts to thwart them. Between missions Duncan frequently travelled home to Edinburgh by motor cycle. On one of these journeys he signalled to make a right-hand turn at a road junction, but a large van behind failed to pass on the signal and as he crossed the road a car travelling very fast pulled out to pass the van. Duncan was thrown off the bicycle as he swung aside, but was unhurt. The car swerved, narrowly missing him, and ploughed through a small hedge into a field, undamaged. The driver jumped out, livid with anger, but calmed down when he surveyed the car saying: 'That's just a miracle!'

'Yes, indeed,' nodded Duncan, meaningfully.

Duncan told no one of his escape, but some months later in a Highland village he was taken to visit a bed-ridden lady whom he had never met before. She surveyed him for a moment and said: 'That's the man I saw in my vision!' Turning to Duncan she added: 'One day you were in great danger. In a vision I saw all hell moved to destroy you and was burdened to pray. At two o'clock in the afternoon the burden lifted and I knew you were safe.' It was the same day and hour on which Duncan had signalled a right-hand turn!

On another trip home he travelled with one of the converts who wanted him to have another interview with

his cousin in Glasgow—the young man who had left the
island so hurriedly after their previous encounter.

The cousin in Glasgow was pleased that his visit to
Skye was now in the realm of almost-forgotten things.
His conscience bothered him from time to time, but
business and pleasure had diverted his attention. He was
sitting in the office when the receptionist announced that
his cousin wished to see him, accompanied by—a Mr.
Campbell! He would have preferred to have seen the
devil!

Assuming an air of defiance he braced himself for the
sermon! His cousin had all the enthusiasm of a new
disciple and exhorted him to change his ways, but to his
amazement Duncan did not preach at all. He just talked
naturally about the mission in Skye, the people he had
met, and the blessings enjoyed.

Was this the same man whose preaching had frightened
him? Duncan's friendliness softened the young fellow's
attitude and he took them for lunch before driving him to
Edinburgh. On the way he talked openly about the things
that would prevent him from living a Christian life. No,
it was not for him.

Duncan pressed the matter no further but simply said
as they parted: 'One day you will change your mind, and
your ways, and when you do, write and let me know.'

For the second time he left Duncan Campbell and
went back to Glasgow to go even deeper into sin. He had
to learn in bitter experience what he had heard in the
paraphrase, that the sinner will be filled with the fruits of
his own ways.

Eventually life became so unbearable that he left the
business and returned to Skye frustrated and empty, the
Word of God continually in his mind. It was hard work
running away from God. The 'Hound of Heaven', 'with

unhurrying chase', was closing the distance between himself and God. Even at the hotel-bar he tried to work off his conviction by preaching to others! One night he picked on a middle-aged man he had never seen before and told him he was a hell-deserving sinner. The man looked frightened. 'Who are you anyway?' he asked.

'Oh, I'm the Church of Scotland missionary from Ardorch,' he lied.

'Well, it's no wonder the church is in the state it is!' the man replied, and left the hotel.

At last the prodigal came to himself. One Sunday morning, broken and dejected, he sent for his cousin who read to him from John's gospel and as they prayed together a great peace came over him; his burden lifted and new hope in Christ filled the horizon. He wrote to Duncan immediately.

Years passed, and one day a woman in Skye looked out, and coming down the path saw a familiar-looking young fellow wearing a minister's collar. Duncan later received another letter inviting him to his pulpit to preach the gospel!

CHAPTER THIRTEEN

Lewis: A Covenant Engagement

WHILE Duncan was in Skye, signs of spiritual awakening were beginning to appear on the Island of Lewis and Harris, the largest of the Outer Hebridean group.

The people of Lewis were no strangers to revivals. Since 1828, when the whole island was shaken out of the slumber of superstition and formalism through the preaching of Rev. Alexander Macleod, Lewis had experienced repeated visitations of the Spirit of God. As a result it was perhaps the most favoured spot in Scotland, as far as sound evangelical witness was concerned. From the pulpits of three Presbyterian denominations the doctrines of the Reformed faith were vigorously proclaimed.

But alongside regular church activity was an equally active godlessness. The town of Stornoway had one of the highest drinking rates in Scotland and 'bothans', illegal drinking-houses, flourished throughout the island. Many, especially the men folk, who were not disposed to yield to the Christian challenge, drowned serious thoughts in this unholy sea.

The last spiritual movement had taken place in 1938-39, but subsided after the outbreak of the Second

World War which caused an exodus of young people from the island to serve in the armed forces. Many of these returned with a spiritual vacuum in their lives, confused and bewildered by what they had seen in Europe and elsewhere. They found it difficult to settle again, and easy to reject the teaching of childhood.

In 1949 there was also a growing carelessness toward spiritual matters among the younger generation. In the High School some pupils were actually speaking of conversion as 'the plague'—something from which to keep away at all costs.

The Christians longed to see a renewed manifestation of God's power. This was evident in the earnestness of the weekly prayer-meetings and in the conversation of God's people when they met together. A church declaration of that time deplored the low state of vital religion within the bounds of the Presbytery, as well as throughout the land, and appealed especially to the young people seriously to consider the end, should there be no repentance. But as Duncan often said: 'Desire for revival is one thing; confident anticipation that our desire will be fulfilled is another.'

Gradually in many praying hearts concern deepened into a conviction that God's time to favour them with a further outpouring of His Spirit had come. Prayer was intensified and faith encouraged. Expectation grew that something would happen. In one village a minister received a promise from God that there would be a harvest gathered in his congregation. His wife also had a dream, in which she saw a church filled with anxious people and a strange minister in the pulpit.

Further along the coast in a small cottage by the roadside in the village of Barvas lived two elderly women, Peggy and Christine Smith. They were eighty-four and eighty-two years old respectively, and spoke only Gaelic. Peggy was blind and her sister almost bent double with arthritis. Unable to attend public worship, their humble cottage became a sanctuary where they met with God. To them came the promise: 'I will pour water upon him that is thirsty and floods upon the dry ground,' which they pleaded day and night in prayer. One night Peggy had a revelation similar to the dream of the minister's wife: revival was coming and the church of her fathers would be crowded again with young people! She sent for the minister, the Rev. James Murray MacKay, and told him what God had shown her, asking him to call his elders and deacons together for special times of waiting upon God.

For months they prayed, then feeling it was time for action Mr. MacKay planned a mission to the parish during the coming winter. The question was, whom should he invite to preach. The answer came when he met Dr. Tom Fitch at Strathpeffer Convention in September. He was told that Duncan Campbell, a Gaelic-speaking minister working with the Faith Mission, was free to conduct missions in the Highlands. After consulting the elder who accompanied him he was convinced that this was the right leading, and immediately sent a telegram to the Faith Mission Headquarters in Edinburgh. On returning to Lewis he was encouraged to hear that one night in a vision the Lord had revealed to Peggy, not only that revival was coming, but also the identity of the instrument He had chosen to use—the same Duncan Campbell as the one mentioned at Strathpeffer!

In the same district a group of men praying in a barn experienced a foretaste of coming blessing. One night as they waited upon God a young deacon rose and read part of the twenty-fourth Psalm: 'Who shall ascend into the

hill of the Lord? or who shall stand in His holy place?
He that hath clean hands and a pure heart; who hath not
lifted up his soul unto vanity, nor sworn deceitfully. He
shall receive the blessing from the Lord.' Turning to the
others he said: 'Brethren, it seems to me just so much
humbug to be waiting and praying as we are, if we our-
selves are not rightly related to God.' Then lifting his
hands toward heaven he cried: 'Oh God, are *my* hands
clean? Is *my* heart pure?'

He got no further, but fell prostrate to the floor. An
awareness of God filled the barn and a stream of supernatural power was let loose in their lives. They had moved
into a new sphere of God-realisation, believing implicitly
in the promise of revival.

But faith had one more test. The invitation to preach in
Barvas was only one of many that reached Duncan
Campbell from different sources that year. He was already
committed to continuing his work in Skye—in fact he was
arranging a holiday Convention in Broadford for the
following year, and regarded this as confirmation to
remain on Skye. Those at Headquarters, desiring to
lend moral support to his decision, advised him to write
Mr. MacKay saying that he was not free to visit Lewis
that winter but would do so at a later date if the door was
still open.

Meanwhile, Duncan had second thoughts! He felt now
that there was something different about the appeal from
Barvas and was inclined to accept it; a reversal of
purpose similar to that of Paul and Timothy when they
assayed to go into Bithynia, but the Spirit suffered them
not' (Acts 16:17).

Those at Headquarters were understandably taken
aback when Duncan informed them that his present
leading and judgment was now contrary to his original

decision, but he concluded, in reply, that he would follow their advice and write Mr. MacKay, 'content to . . . leave the issue in higher hands'.

Higher hands were already at work, engineering circumstances in a way no one could have foreseen; that is with the exception of Peggy—she knew God's secrets. When Mr. MacKay told her that a second appeal to Duncan had produced no further response and that he was unable to come, she replied: 'That's what man says; God has said otherwise! Write again! He will be here within a fortnight!'

A sudden, dramatic change of circumstances took place. A letter reached Duncan to say that the special speaker booked for the Convention in Skye was no longer available. This was followed by news that the Tourist Board had monopolised all accommodation for a festive week during the period in which the Convention was to be held. Freedom from this responsibility was taken as final guidance to accept the invitation to Barvas, and within two weeks Duncan was on the *Loch Seaforth* crossing the Minch to Lewis.

He planned to preach for ten days in Barvas and return to Skye after a short break in Edinburgh. On the eve of his departure to the island he wrote: 'Looking forward to going to Lewis. I am very tired after a heavy time in Skye, but I shall take a good rest when I get home.' Little did he know what awaited him in Lewis!

The Rev. James MacKay with two of his elders were waiting on the pier in Stornoway, when Duncan trudged wearily down the gangplank wearing a heavy pair of black boots and a coat two sizes too big. He looked pale after a choppy sea crossing. One of the elders wondered if he was fit to preach at all. But his outward appearance was secondary in their thoughts. As they exchanged greetings one asked: 'Mr. Campbell, are you walking with God?'

'Well, at any rate, I can say that I fear God,' said Duncan, rather diffidently.

His first contact with the men of Barvas convinced him that he was in the company of those who were living on a high spiritual plane. As he walked down the village road next day his sensitive spirit quickly discerned that God was at work; he realised that revival had already come; it would be his privilege to share in it.

That night he preached from Mathew 25 on 'the wise virgins', challenging the Christians to their responsibility towards those who were asleep in sin. Dust rose from the pulpit cushion as he warmed up to his subject! 'There's fire here,' mused an elder, who felt so convicted that, instead of going home, he walked across the moor to kneel by a peat-bank and pray that God would meet with him afresh.

A solemn hush came over the church the following night when Duncan turned this time to 'the foolish virgins'. The service closed in a tense silence and the building emptied. As he came down from the pulpit a young deacon raised his hand and moving it in a circle above his head whispered: 'Mr. Campbell, God is hovering over. He is going to break through. I can hear already the rumbling of heaven's chariot-wheels.'

Just then the door opened and an elder beckoned: 'Come and see what's happening!' The entire congregation was lingering outside, reluctant to disperse; others had joined them, drawn from their homes by an irresistible power they had not experienced before. There were looks of deep distress on many faces.

Suddenly a cry pierced the silence; a young man who had remained in the church, burdened to the point of agony for his fellow-men, was pouring out his desire in prayer. He was so overcome that he fell into a trance and, as he lay prostrate on the floor, the congregation swept back into the church. The awful presence of God brought a wave of conviction of sin that caused even mature Christians to feel their sinfulness, bringing groans of distress and prayers of repentance from the unconverted. Strong men were bowed under the weight of sin and cries for mercy were mingled with shouts of joy from others who had passed into life. A mother was standing with her arms around her son, tears of joy streaming down her face, thanking God for his salvation. 'Oh, praise the Lord, you've come at last!' Prayers of years were answered.

Hunger to hear the Word of God was so great that when the service finished in the small hours of the morning, the people assembled again a short distance away in the Police Station, where many found the Saviour.

Peggy and her sister shared in the revival. When the minister visited them the following day they told how they had been battling in prayer the previous night reminding God again of His promise. 'We struggled through the hours of the night refusing to take a denial. Had He not promised and would He not fulfil. Our God is a covenant-keeping God and He must be true to His covenant engagements. Did He fail us? Never! Before the morning light broke we saw the enemy retreating, and our wonderful Lamb taking the field.' On being asked what supported their faith in prayer, Peggy replied: 'We had a consciousness of God that created a confidence in our souls which refused to accept defeat.' Confined as they were to their cottage these sisters prayed through the village. Each home was remembered as they knelt before God, and they were so acquainted with the work of the Spirit that they knew instinctively where anxious souls were to be found.

News of what was happening in Barvas spread faster than the speed of gossip. The following night buses arrived from various parts of the island filled with men and women anxious to see and hear the wonderful work of God. Within a matter of days the whole neighbourhood was powerfully awakened to eternal realities. Work was largely set aside as people became concerned about their own salvation, or the salvation of friends and neighbours. In homes, barns and loom-sheds, by the roadside or the peatstack, men could be found calling upon God and soon the fire spread to other villages as invitations came to visit churches throughout the island.

It is necessary here to point out that in tracing the beginnings of the movement, this account has been confined to events relating specifically to Duncan Campbell and the people of Barvas. In other parts of the island were Christian people who had received similar indications of God's purposes and were also being stirred by the Spirit, if not on the same scale.

But before leaving Peggy and her sister, another story must be told which further illustrates the holy intimacy of this woman with her Lord. When the movement was at its height Peggy sent for Duncan, asking him to go to a small, isolated village to hold a meeting.

The people of this village did not favour the revival and had already made clear their policy of non-involvement. Duncan explained the situation to Peggy and told her that he questioned the wisdom of her request. 'Besides,' he added, 'I have no leadings to go to that place.'

She turned in the direction of his voice, her sightless

eyes seemed to penetrate his soul. 'Mr. Campbell, if you were living as near to God as you ought to be, He would reveal His secrets to you also.'

Duncan felt like a subordinate being reprimanded for defying his general. He humbly accepted the rebuke as from the Lord, and asked if he and Mr. MacKay could spend the morning in prayer with them.

She agreed, and later as they knelt together in the cottage Peggy prayed: 'Lord, You remember what You told me this morning, that in this village You are going to save seven men who will become pillars in the church of my fathers. Lord, I have given Your message to Mr. Campbell and it seems he is not prepared to receive it. Oh Lord, give him wisdom, because he badly needs it!'

'All right, Peggy, I'll go to the village,' said Duncan when they had finished praying.

'You'd better!' she replied. 'And God will give you a congregation.'

Arriving in the village at seven o'clock they found a large bungalow crowded to capacity with many assembled outside. Duncan gave out his text: 'The times of this ignorance God winked at, but now commandeth all men everywhere to repent.' When he had finished preaching a minister beckoned him to the end of the house to speak again to a number of people who were mourning over their sins—among them, Peggy's seven men!

CHAPTER FOURTEEN

Sweeping to Victory

IT is difficult to convey the sense of 'livingness' that prevails in a community where God is working. The very air seems to be tingling with divine vitality. Everything, grass, stones, sea and sky, seems to cry out: 'God is here!' Even a fly, buzzing around a lamp, became God's messenger to a hardened sinner in Lewis. He watched the insect for a moment, then muttered: 'If you go much closer you'll get burned.' The words boomeranged into his soul and in a flash he saw the danger of playing with sin and sought Christ.

Duncan described this revival aura simply and accurately as 'a community saturated with God'. The presense of God was a universal, inescapable fact: at home, in the church, and by the roadside. Many who visited Lewis during this period became vividly conscious of the spiritual atmosphere before they reached the island.

> From Thy Spirit whither shall I go,
> Or from Thy presence fly?

was sung with a new depth of meaning. One night a man came to a manse in great concern. The minister brought him into the study and asked: 'What touched you? I haven't seen you at any of the services.'

'No,' he replied, 'I haven't been to church but this revival is in the air. I can't get away from the Spirit.'

Those who tried to run from Christianity for years found themselves shut in with God as the story of a young man on the east side of the island illustrates. His sister had been to Barvas and brought back word of what was happening. He was frightened and in his own way actually prayed that God would keep this man Campbell away from the village where he lived; *he* didn't want to be converted! But Duncan came. For a few nights the man refused to attend but eventually gave in. One night the speaker referred to those who had made vows to serve God when in danger at sea but had not fulfilled them. 'That's me!' he said to himself; his boat had been torpedoed during the war. 'My sister must have told him about me. I'll settle with her when I get out!'

But conviction seized him, and increased next day when Duncan visited his home and prayed with him. By evening the burden of sin was unbearable and at the service when Duncan asked seekers to meet him in the vestry for prayer, he was ready to scramble over the crowds to get there!

Duncan prayed with him and pointed him to the Scriptures but he could not grasp the message of salvation. Despairingly he thought: 'I'm lost, really lost! There's nothing but hell for me!' His whole being seemed suspended between heaven and hell.

At last Duncan said: 'I think you had better pray yourself.'

'But I have no prayer,' he objected.

'Then just ask the Lord for mercy.'

He fell on his knees and uttered only a few words

when the miracle happened. The intolerable burden slipped away and the joy of forgiveness flooded in. Looking down he seemed to see materialised on the floor the locks and chains of sin which had bound him. He leaped up in an ecstasy of love to Christ thinking that he was going straight to heaven. Later as he met an elder by the roadside, a circle of light seemed to envelop them, and looking up to locate its source he found himself gazing into the face of his Saviour.

Not all conversions were so vivid and spectacular but such testimonies were not uncommon.

Spiritual sensitivity greatly increased. 'Have you done business with God today?' was a frequent greeting by the roadside. Christians were instinctively drawn to homes where others were praying, or where someone was seeking the Lord. A woman milking a cow was moved by God to go immediately and plead with a neighbour to yield to Christ; a young man driving a bus was burdened to stop and plead with the passengers to repent, sure that someone was hearing God's voice for the last time and would not be returning with them; but the warning went unheeded, and before the return journey, a young man died in tragic circumstances.

As the revival continued, no one was more sensitive to the movings of the Spirit than Duncan himself. A minister with whom he stayed related that he often knew beforehand who was going to be saved. One day, looking across a loch to a house on the other side, he remarked to his companion: 'Donald, there's a young woman who is going to find the Saviour in that house tonight.' It happened exactly as he said.

A prayer-warrior who lived miles away from Tarbert was able to say when the movement reached that village. Naming the time and date he said: 'I was in the barn when suddenly the place was flooded with light, and I felt that God had broken through in Tarbert.'

'You're right,' said the missionary to whom he was speaking, 'That was the hour when God swept through the meeting and many were converted.'

Sense of time and tiredness vanished as the life-giving Spirit energised those involved in the movement. House meetings continued throughout the night, but sleep was impossible or undesirable; it seemed a waste of time in such an atmosphere. One night two young women were sitting dozing on the stairs of a crowded house, but as an elder prayed the Spirit fell upon the gathering, jerking them awake as though they had been struck with lightning. One who had been reluctant to go to the service was smitten with conviction of sin and cried out so loudly that she had to be taken to a room where she was pointed to the Saviour. A schoolmaster, also a man of prayer, continued for weeks with only a couple of hours sleep snatched after classes each day. Groups of converts, unwilling to go home, would gather on the roadside or the sea-shore singing praises to God and sharing together what He had done for them. One night in Ness the crowd was so great that they spilled out of the house into a field and sang until it seemed the angels were joining with them. An old woman, bitterly opposed to the revival, came out of a nearby house and shouted angrily at the first man she met: 'I wish you would go away home and give people peace to sleep.'

Towering over her this big fellow placed his hands on her shoulders and replied: 'Go away home yourself, *cailleach*, you've been asleep long enough!' She took fright and hobbled back into the house as fast as her rheumatics would allow.

Duncan often complained about being tired, but was

repeatedly quickened in body to meet the heavy demands placed upon him as the fire spread from place to place. Remarkable too was the guidance he received concerning what to preach. He believed in diligent preparation of sermons under normal circumstances, but in the revival had little time for preparing addresses, and with house meetings often arranged spontaneously he never knew what would be required. Frequently a verse of Scripture quoted in prayer would spark off an impromptu address exactly suited to the needs of those present.

An instance of the amazing guidance he received occurred one night when a lorry engaged to convey a number of people to the service broke down. Still seven miles from the village, the younger members of the party decided to walk, but older ones reluctantly retraced their steps. However, the road wound round the end of a loch, and it suddenly occurred to them that if a boat could be found they would still be in time for a later meeting. Three miles back a small boat was available so they crossed the loch to find a meeting in progress. Duncan, knowing nothing of their experience, announced his text: 'They also took shipping and came to Capernaum, seeking for Jesus.' They too were seeking for Jesus and found Him that night. As dawn was breaking a large crowd accompanied them to the shore and they set sail for home amid singing and rejoicing.

Three teenage girls became concerned and started to read the Bible together. They didn't want anyone to know, so they kept handy a copy of *The People's Friend*. If anyone came into the room the Bible was whisked out of sight: they were reading *The People's Friend*! One night they were sitting together in church when Duncan pointed directly at them and said: 'You're in the meeting tonight, and you've got *The People's Friend* in one hand

and the Bible in the other.' They were stunned and
solemn. Surely only God had told him that.

One of the most notorious drunkards on the island
was persuaded to hear Duncan preach in Leurbost and
received a word-picture of his character. He came out
in a rage blaming an old elder for telling the minister
about him. Next day he went drinking to keep away from
'those Christian fools'. But he was disturbed; something
had touched him the previous night; he had caught the
curam (the term Gaelic speakers use to describe someone
who has come under conviction of sin). Chased home by
the police, after being reported as drunk in charge of a
vehicle, he went to a friend's house and with a bottle of
whisky in his hand jumped on a chair to imitate Duncan
preaching; but next morning he awoke out of his stupor
under a terrible burden of sin. He thought there was no
hope for him and that, if he met Christ, it would be as a
Man of wrath who would put him into hell immediately.
Terribly afraid of Christ, and more afraid to die, he
decided he had nothing to lose by going to another
service. Duncan had moved to the village of Arnol, on
the other side of the island, so he started out across the
moor with another young man, and at Barvas asked
directions of a policeman. Amazed at himself he thought:
'Something has happened to me! Here I am, seeking a
minister and talking to a policeman!'—the two men he
hated most in the world.

They went on, not knowing where the service would be
held, but arrived at the very house and entered by the
back door. Duncan was preaching in the front hallway
and the first thing he heard was: 'You are here tonight
and you are afraid of Christ. And the Christ you are
afraid of loves you more than your mother ever did, and
will awaken you from the slumber of death with His

gentle, loving hand. He is waiting now to receive you.'

What a surprise! Could it be true? Did Christ love him after all? He reached home at two o'clock in the morning, went to the loom-shed, and, on his face on the floor, asked Christ to take his life and do with it as He pleased. His fears vanished and the Saviour came in bringing peace and deliverance.

Duncan preached the same sermons often, occasionally several times in one night. Seeing an elder from Stornoway in a service, who had been at a previous one over twenty miles away, he was a little embarrassed and said: 'I'm afraid you are going to have to listen to the same word again.'

'Oh don't worry about that, Mr. Campbell', replied the other comfortingly, 'just you carry on. I'm an angler, and I would never dream of throwing away a fly the fish are taking.'

There was nothing complicated about Duncan's preaching. It was fearless and uncompromising. He exposed sin in its ugliness and dwelt at length on the consequences of living and dying without Christ. With a penetrating gaze on the congregation, and perspiration streaming down his face, he set before men and women the way of life and the way of death. It was a solemn thought to him that the eternity of his hearers might turn upon his faithfulness. He was standing before his fellowmen in Christ's stead and could be neither perfunctory nor formal. His words were not just a repetition of accumulated ideas, but the expression of his whole being; he gave the impression of preaching with his entire personality, not merely with his voice.

It was prophetic preaching, not diplomatic, and the hearers were called to make a clear choice, for there was no middle path. During the revival the wrath of God was

emphasised and coming judgment. God had given him
this emphasis. Once he tried to be more pleasing in the
presentation of truth but without effect and in spite of
constant criticism continued to press the flaming sword
into the very heart of the foe, resisting every effort
to make him retreat. Leaving a service one night after
listening to a famous preacher who was noted for his
'positive gospel', he found himself beside another
minister who had often censured his messages. The
sermon they had listened to was on Paul's word to the
Philippian jailor: 'Believe on the Lord Jesus Christ
and thou shalt be saved.'

'What did you think of that?' his critic asked. 'No
telling *him* to flee from wrath to come!'

'Maybe not,' replied Duncan slowly 'but you must
remember that the dear man was already in full flight.'

While he thundered the judgments of God unsparingly
on those who continued in sin, there was a beautiful
tenderness when he addressed those seeking Christ in
true repentance. The jewel of grace shone more brightly
against the backcloth of law and judgment. Indeed, those
who listened sometimes saw his countenance glow with
light as he dwelt on the love of Christ and God's welcome
to returning sinners.

Undoubtedly the insistence on a true knowledge of sin
and genuine repentance was one of the reasons for the
deep conviction of sin which characterised the movement.
At times the preacher's voice was drowned with the sound
of men and women weeping uncontrollably; on occasions
he found it necessary to stop preaching because of the
distress manifested by those whose consciences had been
awakened. Men, broken in spirit, wept openly over their
sin. Here is one working at peats on the moor and
suddenly bursts into a flood of tears. 'Why am I crying?'

he asks 'I didn't used to be so soft.' He remembers the two ships that had gone down under him at Dunkirk and he had shown no fear; now he trembles. Hastening home he goes to the barn and yields with the prayer: 'Oh God if it's my surrender You want, You've got it now.'

Another, who had been given up by the ministers as totally indifferent, is cycling along the road with the Word of God pounding in his brain causing him to dismount; it seems that hell has opened up, spitting out balls of fire on the road before him.

In the fields, or at the weaving looms, men were overcome and prostrated on the ground before God. One said: 'The grass beneath my feet and the rocks around me seem to cry: "Flee to Christ for refuge!"'

The agony of conviction was terrible to behold, but Duncan rejoiced knowing that out of the deep travail would be born a rich, virile Christian experience, unlike the cheap, easy-going 'believism' that produces no radical moral change. An old man underlined this in his prayer when he said bluntly: 'Lord, now that You have us in the big pot, boil us well!'

A Christian woman showed her distaste for premature professions when her husband came under conviction. Distressed and unable to sleep he walked the roads day and night asking everyone to pray for him. Then an elder, fearing the man was losing his sanity, asked Duncan to visit him. Arriving at the croft in the early hours of the morning, after returning from a service in another village, he found a prayer-meeting in progress in the kitchen. 'I understand your husband is in distress of soul,' he said to his wife.

'It's about time, it's about time,' she replied, and took him to the bedroom door.

Her husband was kneeling at the bedside with his head in his hands, unconscious of their presence, crying: 'O God, hell is too good for me! Hell is too good for me!'

She waited a moment, then closed the door determinedly. 'There he is, Mr. Campbell, there he is, the mighty sinner! Let him take his bellyful!' Crude language! But she was only anxious that God would do a deep lasting work in her husband's life. Next morning prayer was answered, when the overwhelming peace and joy of pardon reached him.

Duncan knew the danger of allowing human sympathy to interfere with the work of the Spirit and offered no superficial comfort to those in distress. He was called one night to the house of a young woman who was so perturbed that the local doctor certified her as insane and advised taking her to hospital. The girl was under the impression that she had committed the unpardonable sin and when Duncan entered the room she screamed: 'God has forsaken me. My soul is going to be with the devil!'

Duncan, prompted by the Spirit, replied: 'I'm glad to hear you say that.'

'How can you ... Mr. Campbell?' interrupted the distraught father. 'How can you say that, when she's in such a state?'

'Well,' Duncan explained, 'when God leaves a soul, He takes His fear with Him, but she still has the fear of God if she is afraid of being forsaken.'

Instantly, the hope of mercy dawned upon the girl; she looked to the Cross and found release. Her spiritual bands unloosed and her tortured mind at rest, the overjoyed father sent word to the doctor saying: 'What medicine could not do, grace has accomplished!'

CHAPTER FIFTEEN

'Swordsmen All'

'WHAT'S the atmosphere like in the parish?' Duncan asked the Rev. Angus MacFarlane, as they were about to start a mission in his church.

'Well, I think it's ready for a match,' Angus replied.

'I agree with your assessment,' Duncan commented after the first meeting. There was a spirit of expectancy. But the nights passed and to their disappointment nothing happened. Duncan contacted a group of men in Barvas, requesting their prayers, and also gave himself to prayer.

One afternoon the minister was mowing hay on the glebe. Duncan was in the study. Suddenly he came running out waving his arms and shouting excitedly: 'It's coming! It's coming! We've got through at last! We're over the top!'

That night revival broke out. God was everywhere. His presence became a living reality, drawing people to church and convicting those who never came near it.

The presence of praying men was a great encouragement to Duncan when he was preaching. At the commencement of each mission he believed in getting those who had already been involved in revival to come to the services.

'But surely, Mr. Campbell, you don't think revival is contagious?' one minister said.

'No,' he replied, 'but these are people who have witnessed the movings of God. They are men filled with the Holy Spirit and the spiritual influence of their presence and prayers can help.'

Duncan was putting into practice the lessons in teamwork learned in the army. Co-ordinated effort, especially in prayer, was necessary if victory was to be won. He played down his own part in the revival, pointing out that revival had come to Lewis before he arrived, and attributed the success of the movement to the faithful preaching of others, who had sown the seed during the years prior to the revival, and to the ministers who assisted him.

But he valued most those who laboured in prayer. It was vital to have covering support in prayer when engaged in spiritual advance, and when encountering opposition and difficulties he would gather a group of men together to intercede. 'More was wrought through the prayers of these men than all the ministers put together, including myself,' he stated.

In Arnol many of the people remained aloof when a mission commenced in the village, and also at this time opposition to the revival was being raised in other parts of the island. An evening was given to waiting upon God in the home of an elder. Around midnight Duncan turned to the local blacksmith: 'John, I feel the time has come for you to pray.'

With his cap in his hand John rose to pray, and in the middle of his prayer he paused, raised his right hand to heaven, and said: 'O God, You made a promise to pour water upon him that is thirsty and floods upon the dry ground, and, Lord, it's not happening.' He paused again and then continued: 'Lord, I don't know how the others here stand in Your presence; I don't know how the ministers stand, but, Lord, if I know anything about my own heart I stand before Thee as an empty vessel, thirsting for Thee and for a manifestation of Thy power.' He halted again and after a moment of tense silence cried: 'O God, Your honour is at stake, and I now challenge You to fulfil your covenant engagement and do what You have promised to do.'

Many who were present witnessed that at that moment the house shook. Dishes rattled in the sideboard, as wave after wave of Divine power swept through the building. A minister standing beside Duncan turned and said: 'Mr. Campbell, an earth tremor!' but Duncan's mind, however, was in the fourth chapter of Acts, where the early Christians were gathered in prayer and, we read: 'When they had prayed the place was shaken where they were assembled together; and they were all filled with the Holy Ghost.'

He pronounced the benediction immediately and walked out to find the community alive with an awareness of God. A stream of blessing was released which brought salvation to many homes during the succeeding nights.

Among those converted the following night was a fifteen-year-old boy who became an outstanding helper in the revival. At school he had heard of the 'epidemic' down the coast—the plague which infected people and they were finished! Out of curiosity he went along and God spoke to him. After hearing God's word he stood outside the house crying: 'I want Christ. I want to get right with God.' Willing hands helped him inside where he found the Saviour. He brought his mother, who was also saved, and then his father, a veteran of the First

World War with shrapnel still under his skin, but without Christ in his heart in spite of vows made to God on the battlefield.

This lad became a 'front-line' prayer-warrior. Duncan called at his home one day and found him on his knees in the barn with the Bible open before him. When interrupted he quietly said: 'Excuse me a little, Mr. Campbell, I'm having an audience with the King.' At school he was ridiculed; one young fellow taunted him with foul language and actually struck him, but with Scriptural meekness he simply turned his head and asked him to strike the other side.

Some of the most vivid outpourings of the Spirit during the revival came when he was asked to pray. In the police station in Barvas he stood up one night, simply clasped his hands together, and uttered one word—'Father.' Everyone was melted to tears as the Presence of God invaded the house. In Callenish, with its ancient Standing Stones he prayed until the power of God laid hold on those who were dead in sins transforming them into living stones in the church of Jesus Christ. But the most outstanding example of God's anointing upon him was in Bernera, a small island off the coast of Lewis. Duncan was assisting at a Communion season; the atmosphere was heavy and preaching difficult, so he sent to Barvas for some of the men to come and assist in prayer. They prayed, but the spiritual bondage persisted, so much so that half way through his address Duncan stopped preaching. Just then he noticed this boy, visibly moved, under a deep burden for souls. He thought: 'That boy is in touch with God and living nearer to the Saviour than I am.' So leaning over the pulpit he said: 'Donald, will you lead us in prayer?'

The lad rose to his feet and in his prayer made reference to the fourth chapter of Revelation, which he had been reading that morning: 'O God, I seem to be gazing through the open door. I see the Lamb in the midst of the Throne, with the keys of death and of hell at his girdle.' He began to sob; then lifting his eyes toward heaven, cried: 'O God, there is power there, let it loose!' With the force of a hurricane the Spirit of God swept into the building and the floodgates of heaven opened. The church resembled a battlefield. On one side many were prostrated over the seats weeping and sighing; on the other side some were affected by throwing their arms in the air in a rigid posture. God had come.

The spiritual impact of this visitation was felt throughout the island; people hitherto indifferent were suddenly arrested and became deeply anxious. The contributor of an article to the local press, referring to the results of this movement, wrote: 'More are attending the weekly prayer-meetings than attended public worship on the Sabbath before the revival.'

God communicated to Peter His purpose to bless the household of Cornelius by means of a vision in a trance when His servant was praying. He used similar methods in Lewis. A young woman in particular repeatedly went into trances, in which she received messages concerning those in need which she passed on to Duncan. One night he was staying in Stornoway when this girl saw in a vision a woman in agony of soul twenty miles away. Duncan was informed that he ought to go and see her, and without any thought for his own rest or safety he motor-cycled to the village and found it exactly as he had been told. The word he spoke brought deliverance, and introduced the troubled lady to the Saviour. Not one message given by this girl through her trance-visions proved false.

This was an aspect of the work which Duncan did not attempt to encourage or explain, but he recognised it was of God and refused to interfere with it, warning those who would associate it with satanic activity, that they were coming perilously near to committing the unpardonable sin.

Another outstanding helper in the revival was the Rev. Murdo MacLennan, the minister in Carloway. With his wife he travelled miles to assist at the services. His great burden was for the young people in his own village. One night at a house-meeting in Barvas he saw two pipers converted who were to have played at a concert and dance in Carloway. He and his wife left immediately for Carloway. On the way he stopped with a group of teenage lads who were coming from the dance and prayed with them in the middle of the road, leaving them amazed and bewildered.

The dance hall was next door to the manse. After a quick cup of tea and prayer together the Lord removed all fears and out they went to the lion's den!

Entertainment at the concert and dance was provided by the Galson Concert Party, a group organised by a schoolmaster and his family. As the minister entered by the side door at 3 a.m. the schoolmaster's wife was the first to meet him. 'I'm sure you're surprised to see me here,' he said.

'Well, I am and I'm not,' she answered; she had heard of some unusual happenings since the revival began.

Just then a young man, immaculately dressed, pushed his way through the curious crowd who had stopped dancing to watch. It was the schoolmaster's son, who was in charge of the proceedings. Usually a quiet, reserved lad he suddenly flamed with anger, bitterly denouncing the intrusion of religion. 'If you want to

come to the dance you should have come through the
main door and paid your entrance fee like everyone else!'
he said. 'You have no authority to come in as you did.'

'As the minister of the parish I have come here with
the authority of my Lord.' This bold reply shook the
young fellow. He wilted under the minister's gaze and
vanished into the crowd, only to reappear a moment
later to apologise for his outburst. Deeply convicted,
he then left the hall and sat weeping in one of the buses
outside.

The minister asked the young people to sing two
verses of a Gaelic Psalm. He then prayed, telling them
what God was doing in Barvas. A solemn silence per-
vaded as he and his wife walked back to the manse.
Efforts to revive the dance ended in failure. The young
M.C. could not be persuaded to enter the hall again even
to get his coat! Within half-an-hour everyone had
dispersed and the lights went out. The concert party was
disbanded that night and all engagements cancelled the
following morning.

The schoolmaster's son appealed to his father for help
but his father didn't know what to do! Turning to his
wife he said: 'Here I am, I've given them everything
material, but can't help them concerning their souls
because I have nothing myself.' He, too, was seized with
conviction.

There was a tremendous upheaval in this family. It
was one of the most unchurched families on the island;
at eleven years old the youngest boy never remembered
being inside a church, but he remembers vividly the
solemn atmosphere in the home next morning. He
watched his mother go to the junk cupboard to bring
out an unused Bible she had bought years before and
hand it to her husband to commence family worship.

This boy became the youngest convert of the revival.

The schoolmaster and his wife found the Saviour and became diligent helpers. The hall where he trained Air Cadets became the scene of one of the most fruitful missions in Lewis.

Tales of other notable characters could be told; 'Swordsmen all, experienced in battle,' as Mr. MacKay described them; men and women whose help and prayers Duncan valued: there was the butcher who prayed until his whole body vibrated with the power of God; the gamekeeper who filled his van nightly with unconverted neighbours and seldom returned home without a convert; the crofter who clenched his fists like a boxer and excused himself to God in prayer in order to command the devil to leave the service; the tweed-merchant whose big, grey lorry transported people from village to village; and the army of ordinary housewives who, regardless of cost in damaged furniture and family comfort, welcomed the invasion of anxious crowds. Looking back to hallowed spots in kitchen or scullery where the great transaction took place, converts gave thanks to God for those who opened their homes that they might open their hearts to the Son of God.

In many respects Duncan Campbell was an individualist, a man of independent mind ploughing a lonely furrow, and seeking to discharge conscientiously before God his calling to preach the gospel. But the tallest pines need the support of others to remain erect and strong; and while head and shoulders above many in spiritual stature, Duncan leaned heavily upon others to strengthen his hands in the battle for souls. In Lewis he found willing helpers.

CHAPTER SIXTEEN

Obstacles Overcome

'BUT DUNCAN, you can't possibly go! You're booked to speak at the closing meeting. The people will be disappointed.'

It was Easter Monday, 1952. Duncan had just given an address at the Faith Mission Convention in Hamilton Road Presbyterian Church, Bangor, when he was suddenly arrested by a conviction that he should leave at once and go to Berneray, a small island off the coast of Harris with a population of about 400 people. Sitting in the pulpit he tried to fight off the insistent urge but the urgency only increased.

Eventually turning to the chairman he said: 'I must leave the Convention and go to Harris immediately.' Objections were valid enough; the chairman reminded him of his commitments for the following night, but Duncan was unrelenting: 'I'm sorry, I must obey the promptings of the Spirit and go at once.'

He left the pulpit to pack his case and the following morning flew from Belfast to Scotland. On Thursday morning he reached Harris and took the ferry to Berneray. He had never been there before and knew no one on the island. The first person he met was a sixteen-year-old boy. 'Could you direct me to the manse, please?'

'The manse is vacant,' the lad replied. 'We have no minister just now. 'The men (the elders) take the services,' and pointing to a house on the hill, added, 'One lives up there.'

Duncan glanced from the hill to his suitcase, then back to the boy. 'Could you please go and tell him that Mr. Campbell has arrived on the island. If he asks what Mr. Campbell, tell him it's the minister who was in Lewis.'

Ten minutes later the boy came back to say that the elder was expecting him, accommodation had been arranged and a service already intimated for nine o'clock that night! God had gone before.

Three days earlier when Duncan was in the pulpit at Bangor, this man was praying in the barn. He had been there most of the day. God had given him a promise: 'I will be as the dew unto Israel,' which he laid hold of in faith, assured that revival was going to sweep the island.

More than that, he was confident that God would send Duncan Campbell. His wife could hear him in the barn: 'Lord, I don't know where he is, but You know, and with You all things are possible. You send him to the island.' So convinced was he that God would bring him in three days time that he made the necessary arrangements for a mission.

The first few services were uninspiring. Duncan felt tired and spiritually out of breath, but the elder adamantly affirmed that revival was at hand.

One evening as they were preparing to leave the church the old man suddenly took his hat off, pointing excitedly in the direction of the congregation which had just left the service: 'Mr. Campbell, see what's

happening! He has come! He has come!' The Spirit
of God had fallen upon the people as they moved down
towards the main road and in a few minutes they were so
gripped with the subduing presence of God that no one
could move any further. Amid sighs and groans from sin-
burdened souls prayer ascended to God on the hillside.
The entire island was shaken into a new awareness of
God as many lives were saved and transformed during
the following days. In this movement there were no
physical prostrations as in Lewis, but the results were as
deep and abiding.

How glad Duncan was that he had responded to the
Spirit's prompting. Had he remained to preach in Bangor
he would never have reached Berneray in time to fulfil
God's agreement with the elder. Obedience, even at the
risk of misunderstanding, reaped its reward.

Duncan never lightly set aside an engagement to
preach, but never hesitated to do so when convinced that
God wanted him elsewhere. This occasional failure to
honour commitments landed him in trouble with those
who had engaged him. For example, during the revival he
had a policy of continuing in a place as long as souls
were being saved, but this displeased ministers with
whom he had prior commitments and led to unfortunate
disagreements.

The most successful strategy of the devil to weaken
the thrust of a movement of God is to introduce contention among God's children. He is particularly careful
to see that minor differences and misunderstandings are
magnified out of all proportion and that mistakes and
failings, which should be quickly forgiven and forgotten,
become festering sores in the body of Christ.

Opposition is to be expected. Counter-attacks from
the devil are experienced in all awakenings where inroads

are being made into his territory. Active opposition has
been an outstanding feature in every revival. Writing a
foreword to Arthur Wallis's book *In the Day of Thy
Power* Mr. Campbell asked readers to ponder well the
contents of a chapter entitled 'A Sign Spoken Against'
and especially the words: 'If we find a revival that is not
spoken against we had better look again to ensure that
it is a revival.'

Tremendous responsibility as well as costly endeavour,
is placed upon any leader in spiritual advance. Human
relationships are easily strained where the work of God
makes heavy demands on a man's time and energy, and
the leader is usually made to 'carry the can' when mistakes and misunderstandings occur. A lady in Lewis,
describing this aspect of the awakening, said: 'When
people are asleep they don't like to be awakened suddenly
and usually strike out at the first person they see—in this
case the preacher!'

Denominationalism was one of the hindrances in
Lewis. Instead of being viewed as something that should
transcend denominational boundaries, the revival
missions were too often regarded as an effort to destroy
them. There is severe inconsistency in our conception of
the church as 'a body' when we fail to accommodate the
different functions of each member. It makes nonsense
of 'fellowship' when those whom God has chosen to
sow and those He has chosen to reap cannot rejoice
together.

In seeking to steer an interdenominational course
Duncan exposed himself to criticism from all denominations. One church accused him of being a proselytising
agent for another, but it was Duncan's practice to direct
those who were influenced by the movement into their
own local churches, knowing that each had an evangelical

tradition. There were unfortunate instances where converts, disillusioned by the reception they received in one church moved elsewhere, but in a letter to the Director of the Mission, Duncan expressed grief concerning this. From other districts he writes of being greatly cheered by the steadfastness of the converts and their loyalty to the churches.

Duncan readily admitted that he himself was not without blame in some of the difficulties that arose. In the enthusiasm of the moment he did not fully appreciate the importance of normal church growth and activity. He could have used his influence more to prevent enthusiasts by-passing church prayer-meetings to attend the revival services. This caused much antagonism.

In yielding to several requests to organise regular interdenominational prayer-meetings in communities where church prayer-meetings flourished, Duncan also believed he acted unwisely. These abortive attempts were misconstrued to accuse him of anti-church activity, and in some cases of aiming eventually to establish a new denomination on the islands—an absurd suggestion, but too readily believed.

Doctrine was another bone of contention. As already stated Duncan was not a trained theologian and intensely disliked theological controversy, but he was shrewd enough to recognise what A. W. Pink points out in his introduction to *The Sovereignty of God*, that in a community where one aspect of the Divine sovereignty and human responsibility question has been particularly emphasised, it is necessary to place emphasis on the other side to secure a balanced outlook. In other places Duncan loved to dwell on the sovereignty of God but in the Highlands, a stronghold of Calvinism, he stressed man's responsibility in his relationship with God and was consequently labelled 'a mad Arminian'. Pamphlets and declarations appeared denouncing 'the subtle sophistries of Arminianism', and for a time the local press carried 'hot' correspondence on the subject. Duncan wisely ignored the accusations, refusing to be drawn into time-consuming debates that would solve nothing and cause more bitterness. He carried on with his work. He was an evangelist and understandably concentrated on freely offering the gospel to sinners, leaving others to debate the deeper doctrines of the faith.

As in everything, financial support also became a thorn in the flesh. From offerings taken at the services, one church generously donated a gift to the Mission Duncan represented. On the 'grapevine' this considerate act was enlarged upon to assume that the Mission's pocket was being lined from Lewis. Before me is a detailed list of contributions Duncan received during his missions and also a list of expenses, of which he kept diligent account, even to his postage stamps; comparison shows a substantial deficit at the end of each quarter which speaks for itself.

A less serious criticism made Duncan rock with laughter and how he loved to re-tell it. Extremists who obviously believed there was virtue in black cloth and long faces took exception to his footwear. One is reported to have said: 'I was out for a walk yesterday and I met the plague. It isn't hard to see that there's no grace in him, you have only to look at his shoes'—they were brown!

Duncan's main source of illustration was from his own life and ministry, and he frequently related in detail the experiences of those influenced by his preaching. High-landers fiercely object to being used as spiritual exhibits and this was sometimes resented. An account, which he gave in Glasgow, of the awakening in a particular area filtered back to those involved and actually led to the cancellation of a mission in the district.

Nevertheless others were blessed and stirred by reports of the revival. Duncan's old gift of story-telling was a tremendous asset. Often carried away with an intensity of feeling that frequently broke into present tense narrative, he re-lived never-to-be-forgotten scenes of Divine visitation. Audiences were lifted into fervent interest as he related vivid accounts of the Lord's work in the lives of individuals and communities.

But the dramatic manner in which he recounted these experiences sometimes left him open to the charge of exaggeration. For example, references to the closing of drinking-houses were interpreted by listeners to mean licensed public houses, and those unfamiliar with Highland geography and local conditions thought of villages in terms equal to the population of villages in the south, rather than the small remote communities they actually are. Also, Duncan's failure to record incidents on paper, his readiness to accept second-hand reports, plus a failing memory did not help in this respect. But even if names and places did get mixed up, and he inadvertently described scenes in Skye which occurred in Lewis, or vice versa, his motive was pure, and God blessed and used the accounts to stir people in many lands to pray for revival.

Many seeming inconsistencies were unavoidably caused by the intense manner in which Duncan entered into the awareness of God's work in times of spiritual quickening, which impinged upon his imagination a more vivid and arresting picture of souls in conflict than the more objective viewer would receive.

Exaggerated reports and misleading statements from

other sources later gained currency in the Christian press. More than once Duncan had to ask editors to refrain from publishing further articles about the revival, and even had to demand the withdrawal of a book written by a gentleman in America who had more imagination than facts at his disposal. In response to numerous requests, and in order to safeguard against further unreliable publications he eventually compiled an official account of the movement in a small booklet, *The Lewis Awakening*.

Problems such as these, causing misunderstanding and strained relationships, were major stumbling-blocks to Duncan's ministry in the Hebrides and contributed to the decline of the movement. But in addition he had other obstacles with which to do battle.

Those singled out by God for prominent use in the advancement of His Kingdom are usually subjected to disciplines beyond the average Christian's experience. Paul had a thorn in the flesh to keep him humble; Duncan had a discipline of darkness. When the revival sun was at its meridian, God permitted a sudden inexplicable darkness to come over his spirit for three months. At night he could hardly sleep, and during the day paced the floor weeping in his affliction. The only relief he had was in the services when the power of the Spirit came upon him to minister the Word, but immediately on returning to his lodgings the veil dropped again. Then one day as he was crying to God for light, a voice seemed to whisper: 'I can trust you now,' and peace came to his soul. By being denied the conscious presence of God his desire was quickened and his heart humbled, preventing him from becoming too familiar with the sunshine until he reached out appreciatively after the least glimmer of Divine light. God was teaching him that he was to seek no personal glory from the work he had been given to do.

He accepted modestly the respect shown to him as a servant of Christ, who had been used by God in a unique way, but his indignation was roused when anything was said about him that would detract from God's glory. Seeing himself billed once as *The Man who brought Revival to the Hebrides* he was scathing in his comment, pointing out that revival was a sovereign act of God and was in the Hebrides before he ever set foot in the place; he was merely an instrument chosen by God for a specific task, at God's appointed time, in God's prepared place.

God's appointments, however, do not exempt us from the disciplines of domestic life, and while often away from home Duncan did not abdicate his responsibilities in this sphere. Painfully conscious of the extra burden placed upon Mrs. Campbell by his absence, and recognising that it was her involvement and sacrifice behind the scenes which made his ministry possible, he took every opportunity to return to Edinburgh to add his advice and affection in seeking to direct and shape the lives of their children.

Travelling also created problems for the preacher—his motor-cycle was as temperamental as the car he had at Balintore. It created problems for others also—keeping out of the way!

Late one night on his way north the chain snapped on a lonely stretch of road through Glenogle. Too tired to push the bike he gathered some heather and slept under a bush until daybreak! In Lewis he was fortunate to escape with minor bruises after a couple of spills; once he struck a ram, and another day ploughed into the back of a lorry on a narrow single-track road.

The big breakdown was in his vocal chords. His voice

had caused anxiety a few times in the past, which was not surprising. He registered a high count on the decibel scale!

Constant preaching in Lewis eventually caused serious damage. One night in Carloway he had just announced the text: 'Mary, the Master is come and calleth for thee,' when his voice gave out completely, being reduced to a hoarse whisper, but even that one verse brought far-reaching blessing; one of the converts was called into a life of fruitful service which took her to many countries.

Duncan returned to Edinburgh, was examined by leading specialists, to be told that he would never preach again. Then a friend advised him to see a Christian voice therapeutist in London, who in his practice also relied on the healing power of God.

When Duncan introduced himself at the clinic, a wee Welshman, with his sleeves rolled up and wearing an apron, surveyed him for a moment and then announced: 'Mr. Campbell you must be born again!'

Warned to expect unusual behaviour, Duncan resisted the temptation to turn on his heel and walk out. Instead he cautiously replied: 'But I have reason to believe that I have been born again.'

'Yes, but your voice must be born again,' was the belated explanation.

The treatment that followed was even more difficult to comprehend. For three days his throat and diaphragm were massaged energetically and he was instructed to walk around the room, and also out in St. James's Park, constantly repeating: 'I want to be a baby! I want to be a baby!'

On the fourth day they went to a large empty church in the city. The little man with a sweep of his hand said: 'Mr. Campbell, this church is full of angels. You are going to preach to me and to them.'

As Duncan entered the pulpit a text flashed into his mind. He opened the Bible and read a few verses, his voice barely audible in the vast building. But as he began to comment on the verse his voice returned in a torrent of words. The little man dropped to his knees in the pew and cried: 'Thank you, Lord, for another miracle.'

When Duncan returned to Lewis those who heard him say that his voice was entirely different. It was a new voice. It had been 'born again', and never again did he have serious trouble with it.

'We might lose a few battles but we're going to win the war!' an old Christian once said. Duncan had a few painful setbacks during the revival but the overall picture is one of outstanding victory. A report in *The Glasgow Herald* states that while ecclesiastical barriers were felt in some districts, the movement as a whole tended to overstep sectarianism; hundreds were converted and Church membership increased in every district.

The following report by Mr. MacKay indicates the extent and depth of the work in the parish of Barvas alone: 'There are more than one hundred souls in this parish whose hearts God has graciously touched since the movement started. God is maintaining them all; not one has gone back. Their daily living is fragrant, their fellowship blessed, their love vital and glowing— as beautiful a progeny of grace as one has ever seen. Many of them are staunchly upholding the cause of Christ in their own home areas; but there are some who are now scattered throughout the world.'

The number of converts who entered the ministry and engaged in the missionary activities of various churches and organisations is proof of the stability and vitality of the work. A minister from Ness, in a letter to a business-man in Edinburgh, wrote: 'I am glad to inform you that the results are very encouraging. The converts are grow-ing in grace and are definitely an asset to the church and community. Their interest in spiritual things is steadily increasing which convinces us that a genuine spiritual awakening has taken place as the result of the stirring preaching of Mr. Campbell.'

And over twenty years later another minister adds that wherever he goes on the island today he finds men and women walking with God who were brought to Christ through Duncan's ministry.

CHAPTER SEVENTEEN

Weapons of War

THE military flavour of Paul's epistles is inescapable. He draws uncompromising battle lines, pinpoints the tactics of the enemy, outlines the Christian's armour, and finally underlines the two essential weapons in aggressive spiritual warfare, the sword of the Spirit, which is the Word of God, and the artillery of prayer. Like Paul, Duncan Campbell proved the effective use of these weapons in revival and encouraged others to arm themselves for battle.

To go to war without these is to court defeat. The army with the better weapons has a decided advantage in conflict. But what use are weapons if the soldier is not trained and equipped to use them properly and skilfully? The Word of God is the Sword *of the Spirit*; prayer is to be always *in the Spirit*. The essential equipment, therefore, for the Christian soldier is the power of the Holy Spirit.

In the Casualty Clearing Station Duncan had witnessed the conquering power of the Word of God when uttered under the anointing of the Spirit. From that time the Bible became to him a living, dynamic book. Its message required no apology and needed none of the gimmicks of quasi-evangelical entertainment. A leader in Christian work trying desperately to maintain the interest of a group of young people who had made decisions in a crusade asked Duncan what entertainment he had provided for the converts in Lewis. 'Entertainment!' exclaimed Duncan. 'They wanted no entertainment. Their desire was to hear the Word of God and attend the prayer-meetings!'

'Preach the Word! Sing the Word! Live the Word!' he declared, 'Anything outside of this has no sanction in heaven!' Religious movies and plays which involved dramatising spiritual truth, and particularly the work of the Holy Spirit, were blasphemy to him. What was wrong with the drama of the Acts of the Apostles? Why do we need a substitute in yards of celluloid and amateur play-acting, if God is still the same, and has promised to impart living faith to men through the spoken word in the power of the Holy Spirit? Why not have the real thing?

This was his challenge. His fear was that the glory had all but departed from the church, and entertainment was necessary to accommodate an age that was more desirous of being amused than instructed in the deep things of God; more concerned about being happy than facing the real implications of Calvary. Christianity was not fun and games. The Bible meant what it said or it did not. If the Bible was true why were its promises not being fulfilled? They could be!

Here is the impression of a student who heard him preach: 'I had been to Bible College but the practical reality of the Word of God had not come through to me. When I heard Duncan Campbell I received a more intelligent faith—a basis to believe that miracles can still happen. His confidence in the Word of God was out-

standing. When he read and explained it, you could just
expect it to happen that way.'

To Duncan Campbell the Bible was not an end in
itself; it was the means to an end. It was the written Word
of God to lead men into a living, experimental relationship with the Living Word, and to guide them in that
relationship. It was not an academic book merely to
study and criticise. Those who used it solely in this way
were handling it to their own damnation. If it was not a
life-giving, transforming, creative Word, it could be an
instrument of death. It must be heard and studied with a
view to obedience, and obedience would lead to new life
in the Spirit. Therefore it must be preached in the Spirit.

Duncan often quoted Paul's words: 'The letter killeth,
but the Spirit giveth life.' He was afraid lest he should
'help the devil to damn souls by quoting Scripture in
the energy of the flesh'.

The dream of a Puritan preacher who saw the devil
proclaiming the Gospel on the street corner was a
personal reminder to Duncan of this dangerous possibility. The Puritan astounded at seeing such an unexpected
evangelical orator, asked: 'Aren't you the devil?'

'Yes.'

'But why are you preaching the gospel? I thought your
business was to damn souls, not to save them.'

'Yes,' replied the devil, 'but I have discovered that the
best way to achieve my ends is by preaching the gospel
without the anointing of the Holy Spirit.'

An experience in counselling emphasised to Duncan
the need for the Holy Spirit to illumine His own Word to
hearers and, he said, rebuked him for lack of dependence
on the Holy Spirit. He was asked to visit a home where a
young woman was distressed about her soul, and after
quoting a few invitations and promises from the Bible,

he waited for a word of assent. The girl looked at him silently, then said: 'But Mr. Campbell, surely you don't think that believing a verse of Scripture can save me?'

He shuddered when listening to an evangelist ask a group of enquirers at a campaign if they believed a certain verse, and on receiving a favourable reply, he concluded: 'Now you are saved!'

Duncan sought to avoid the snare of underestimating the power of the Word of God on the one hand, and the danger of overstating the function of Scripture on the other. The Word of God is like a hammer that breaks the rock, to remove prejudice and rebellion; it is like a fire, to melt and slacken the icy grip of unbelief; it is like a sword to pierce and open the wounds of sin. In short, it can show men they need to be saved; it can direct them to the Saviour, it can assure them of salvation, but it *cannot* save. Only an encounter with the living Christ can do that.

He kept his argument and appeal rooted in the Word. The President of Prairie Bible Institute, Rev. L. E. Maxwell, writes of him: 'There was nothing light or frothy about his appeal. He was deep in the Word and based his message upon the infallible Book.'

Like Rowland Hill he could have been charged with wandering from Dan to Beersheba during the course of a sermon, he quoted so many Scriptures, but could equally have replied: 'I know that, but I kept on holy ground!'

He was a man of one Book. Not that he was unfamiliar with other literature. Quotations from a wide range of theologians and preachers betrayed his acquaintance with them, but the Bible was unique—supreme. He rejoiced to see men tremble at the Word of God.

A professor of theology of the Barthian School asked him to what he attributed the success and stability of his work in the Highlands of Scotland when his preaching did not achieve similar results in the Lowlands. He replied fearlessly: 'Because I was speaking to people who believed in the infallibility and inspiration of every word of Scripture, and who were prepared to act upon it.'

Prayer was as important to Duncan as preaching. One was complementary to the other. It has already been pointed out that he regarded prayer as indispensable to break down opposition before victory could be achieved.

Free-lance village evangelism in his early Christian life taught him never to miss an opportunity to talk to men and women about God, but he also learned then that it is much more important to speak to God about men. A friend and colleague of many years tells us that he not only ardently believed in prayer, he practised it, and in this laid the sure foundation for his successful missions.

He spent hours in prayer. At *Camus-liath* he had recourse to the barn where he had offered his first prayer of faith, and throughout his life private prayer and family devotions were not only important, they were imperative. One morning as he was about to commence family worship one of the children said: 'Daddy, do we have to have the reading every day, *every day*?'

With equal emphasis, he replied, 'Do you have to have your food every day, *every day*?'

His elder daughter tells another amusing story which indicates the impression which his prayer-life had upon the family: 'One evening when Sheena and John were small children, a great volume of sound descended from the bedroom. In spite of several warnings the noise continued. When Dad went upstairs, intent on disciplinary action, he found two little forms piously kneeling with folded hands. They felt that his respect for prayer was a sure shield from punishment!'

The prayer life must be fought for, he insisted; everything will militate against it. The world with its pressures and speed will give us no time; the flesh with its appetites and weaknesses will rob us of concentration; Satan will concentrate his subtle powers to contend every inch of the prayer-route. The tide of battle turns in the closet; this is where the real warfare is accomplished. It is there Satan is served with an authoritative notice to quit.

For this reason the most vital part of the day to Duncan Campbell was the morning-watch. It was an unusual circumstance that found him in bed after six o'clock. He heard the advice which Dr. Stuart Holden's mother wrote on the fly-leaf of her son's Bible at his ordination: 'Begin the day with God. See His face first, before you see the face of another.'

Duncan took this advice to himself and made it a life-long habit. At the break of day he could hear the crofters harnessing the horses to the plough to turn the sods and sow the grain in anticipation of harvest. If men could rise early and work hard for earthly gain, he could not understand why Christians could lie in bed with a harvest of souls to be reaped, and obstacles to be removed by prayer. 'Give the best hours of the day to God,' he would say.

The discipline of keeping the morning-watch was not only a duty, it was a delight. What thirst for God was created in other lives when he shared the blessings of fellowship with the Saviour in those morning hours! Then to tempt others to follow his example he would quietly ask: 'Who wouldn't get up to be in such company?'

It required discipline to win this battle. It must be won the night before, he maintained, and often excused himself from an evening of enjoyable fellowship in order

to get to bed and rise early to keep his appointment with
the One he loved the most.

On the fly-leaf of his own Bible he inscribed words of
the late Lieutenant-General Sir William Dobbie: 'I have
never found anything to compare with this morning-
watch as a source of blessing, when one meets God
before meeting the world. It is a good thing to speak to
Him before we speak to other people, to listen to His
word before we listen to the voices of our fellow-men.'

During these hours of communion with God the fresh
dew of heaven bathed his soul, refreshing and equipping
him for daily service. He carried the fragrance of the
presence of God with him from the secret place into his
public ministry. The voice of the Saviour, heard so
clearly in the early stillness, was not only sweet to his
own taste but was a word in season for those who looked
to him for guidance and counsel.

As a spiritual counsellor he was unequalled, and the
secret of his valued advice was the open ear he had for
God's Word when praying about any particular situation.
He carried no list of proof-texts or neat arguments to
meet possible needs, but always had a relevant word from
God concerning problems confided in him. He lived near
to God and sometimes God spoke to him about the needs
of others before he was told of them at all.

On one occasion a young worker conducting a mission
with him was experiencing a trying time of oppression
from the enemy. Doubts haunted him. A terrible dread
stalked through his thoughts robbing him of peace and
assurance. No one knew of his condition. At the morning
fellowship in the manse Duncan usually asked him to
read the portion for the day. This particular morning
he chose to read himself and opened the Bible at the
thirty-fourth Psalm. When he reached verse four: 'I

sought the Lord, and He heard me, and delivered me from all my fears,' the Spirit of God immediately came upon the young fellow with instant release. The impact was felt not only in the prayer-meeting which followed but in the two services that evening.

When they returned to the manse for supper he told Duncan what had happened. In his simple, humble manner, Duncan merely replied: 'Yes I know. The Lord gave me that word for you when I was praying this morning!'

Another day a friend was passing through a period of spiritual darkness and depression. Duncan, having his customary afternoon rest, was lying meditating and praying, when a verse came vividly to his mind and a voice told him to take it to his friend. He went immediately and the word brought light and comfort to a troubled mind.

Duncan learned how to prevail in prayer. When the burden of prayer was upon him for a district he often prayed throughout the day instead of visiting. During the revival a lady, who lived in a croft near where he was staying, sometimes woke up in the middle of the night and from the back door could hear him still engaged in prayer after a strenuous day.

Reports sent in from missions indicate the intensity with which he prayed through to victory: 'I am going through the fire. May the Lord help me. Had a most blessed night of prayer and waiting upon God.'

'A very stiff fight here, but there are signs that the opposition is yielding. We shall yet see victory.'

'A week of hard fighting against the wind, rain and the devil! At the prayer-meeting tonight we felt that the tide of battle had changed. Strong men were visibly moved in the grip of conviction.'

'Revival has come! I have witnessed soul-stirring scenes since the break came on Monday night. There has been a stream of blessing since. The struggle leading to this glorious crisis was such as I have seldom, if ever, encountered. But God be praised, He enabled us to press through to victory until we saw the ramparts of hell crumbling before His mighty power.'

'The weapons of our warfare are not carnal but mighty through God to the pulling down of strongholds.' So wrote Paul. Spiritual warfare requires spiritual weapons, and spiritual weapons are only effective in the hands of Spirit-filled men, and Duncan Campbell, whatever his limitations in other spheres, was a man 'filled with the Holy Ghost'.

CHAPTER EIGHTEEN

Spreading the Flame

THE inspiration of being in revival added a new attraction to Duncan's preaching. In response to invitations from churches and other Christian organisations he travelled extensively throughout the British Isles and farther afield, never sparing himself, and finding it difficult to refuse any request for service, until the Mission eventually formed a small committee to handle his engagements as a safeguard against overbooking—and double booking!

But nothing could compare with returning to the Highlands and Islands to minister again in Gaelic. He loved to visit the Pilgrims in these regions and had the privilege of sharing with them in movements of the Spirit. From the Island of North Uist they sent for him when the battle was tough, but he arrived after a stormy sea-crossing too ill to preach. A few days in bed, and he joined in the fight to witness memorable scenes of Divine power. Many young men and women were converted; one describes what happened as God's servant preached:

> My past life was brought before me, and the terrible consequences of neglecting Christ. I promised the Lord that whatever others would do I would give my

heart to him. In fear and trembling I waited for the 'after-meeting' to join God's people in prayer and then four days later lying in bed the burden of sin rolled away. I knew that I was forgiven and the peace and joy of the Holy Spirit filled my heart.

Two converts from Uist after training in the Faith Mission Bible College returned to the Hebrides to preach, and often enjoyed the privilege of fighting with the 'old soldier', as they affectionately called him.

After the revival in Lewis, Duncan started an annual Convention in Stornoway to which he looked forward each year with the eagerness of a schoolboy; it refreshed his spirit to meet the converts again, some of whom he had not known before. Two women spoke to him on the street one day and after some hesitation he said: 'I'm afraid I don't recognise you. Which parish do you come from?'

'Well, well, Mr. Campbell, you're a strange father! You don't even know your own children,' they chided, and then told how they had been saved in one of his missions.

He never left the island without visiting the praying men, who had meant so much to him in the revival, and with whom he had such affinity of spirit. He marvelled at their discernment and world-wide vision in this far north-western island. Calling to see one of them he arrived at the house to hear him in the barn praying for Greece. He could not understand what interest a butcher in Lewis could have in Greece.

'How did you come to be praying for Greece today?' he asked him later. 'Do you know where Greece is?'

'No, Mr. Campbell, but God knows, and He told me this morning to pray for Greece!'

Two years later Duncan was introduced to a man in Dublin who told him the following story. He had gone to Greece on a business trip and was asked to speak to an assembly of Christians. The Spirit of God worked so powerfully that he continued preaching for a few weeks and phoned his brother in Ireland with instructions to look after the business until he returned. Duncan compared dates and discovered that the movement in Greece began on the same day that the butcher was praying in Barvas!

The prayers of these men followed him through varied situations in which people were brought into new paths of obedience to God. From Croydon he writes: 'Last night the crowd was so great that the service had to be relayed to an adjoining hall, and at the close I dealt with several who were seeking God. One businessman, a local preacher, was in great distress; God had spoken to him about valuable articles which he had stolen years before his conversion and were still in his home. He came at last to the place where he was willing to do the right thing.'

Cases of restitution frequently followed his preaching. A farmer in Ireland came to see him after a church service. 'Mr. Campbell, when you were preaching all I could hear was the barking of a puppy.'

'A puppy?' said Duncan, puzzled. 'I heard no dogs in the church.'

'No, Mr. Campbell, you didn't hear it,' he explained, 'It was barking at the ear of my soul. Years ago when I was a lad I stole a puppy from a farmer, took it across the border, and sold it for five pounds. He is now dead but I must go to his widow and pay back the five pounds with interest.'

Several sought the Lord during a mission in Shetland,

including a young man who rose in the middle of the address and knelt at the front. 'I had to do it,' he said. 'Jesus came so near, I was afraid he would pass by before I reached Him.' A similar incident occurred in Sunderland when a man knelt at the communion rail, to be followed by eighteen others before Duncan had finished preaching.

At a meeting of ministers in Birmingham the sacrifice of a broken spirit was offered to God when many fell to their knees confessing sin and seeking spiritual renewal. But not all appreciated Duncan's message. At another fraternal he had just finished speaking on revival, when one stood up and said: 'Brethren we want revival, but God save us from that!' He was regarded as old-fashioned and told that he should have lived a hundred years ago! A lady suggested that because he was born and brought up in the hills of Scotland he was consequently a bit mystical!

A minister described his preaching as 'kill-joy stuff', but interestingly enough, the young folk whose joys he was supposed to be killing, were those who appreciated most the ring of reality and challenge to godly, sacrificial living which he presented. Scores of young lives were transformed and dedicated to the service of God. Here is what some of them thought about him: 'If you didn't believe in God you could no longer be an atheist after meeting that man. You could see Jesus in his life and touch Jesus in his ministry.'

'He was a gentleman of God. He could afford to be gentle with the strong power that lay behind. There was a paradox of power and humility in his character that impressed me.'

'He focused the light upon God, and this changed my whole way of looking at things. He showed me that God was alive and active and could work in me and through me.'

'Mr. Campbell's ministry cost me a lot, over 10,000 dollars in fact! I had to go back to the United States where I was born and work for a year to make restitution for things I had done as a sinner.'

'He was straightforward, no beating about the bush. I saw what revival really was, that it must begin in me; that I must be rightly related to God.'

Churches were revived as complacent church members were shaken into life, and many who had only a name to live realised that they had never been truly born again. A minister in Glasgow stated that during his twenty-five years ministry there, Duncan Campbell's visit was the high-water mark in the life of his church.

The central theme of the message was holiness of life. 'Revival must ever be related to holiness,' he declared. 'True revival is a revival of holiness.' Personal holiness is more desirable than happiness, he taught, and it is not in heaven alone that God wants our saintliness, it is here and now; holiness is not just a doctrine to be taught, it is a way of life—it is the life of Jesus. It means taking the view that Jesus would take in any course of action, and making that the ruling principle of our lives. This was how he himself sought to live. When the will of his heavenly Commander was clear, neither the offer of personal comfort, nor the opinions of others could weaken his determination to obey. That resolve became the ruling passion of his life; he saw himself as one entrusted to manifest God's character in the world, and must fight to 'guard the deposit'.

When Duncan referred to feeling 'as pure as an angel' after his encounter with God on the battlefield, it must be understood that he was merely stating his own feelings at that time, and not a fact of experience which brought him into a realm of 'sinless perfection'. He was accused of teaching 'sinless perfection' once, perhaps because such statements were misunderstood, but he was quick to bring back to earth any who presumed that they had sprouted wings and sported halos. Hearing a certain gentleman boasting that he had not sinned for forty years, Duncan, with a subtle thrust, replied: 'Well, brother, you have just broken your record!'

He believed in a definite experience of the Spirit subsequent to conversion, but to him there was no experience that finalised the work of sanctification this side of heaven. He wrote: 'Sanctification is a process. The germinal principle is essentially "growable". There must be a gradual development of the Christian character.'

The Holy Spirit brings, as He did on the Day of Pentecost, heart purity, introducing the believer to a cleansed life, but this life is conditioned by walking in the Spirit that the lusts of the flesh might not be fulfilled. Duncan testified that the nearer he came to God the more he discovered things in his life, which he never suspected before, requiring forgiveness and cleansing.

This subsequent experience he preached as 'the baptism' or 'fullness of the Holy Spirit', and pointed out that in its final analysis it was a new revelation of Jesus. All impressions produced by the Holy Spirit should lead to the life of the Lord Jesus being reproduced in the believer, and this, rather than supernatural gifts, is evidence of the validity of spiritual experience.

Overwhelmed with the excellency of Christ's redeeming work, he desired the presence of Jesus more than anything else; at times Jesus was more real to him than his earthly friends and those who met him became conscious of it. Ministers, students, housewives and fishermen speak of this as the arresting feature of his personality.

It was to see this purpose fulfilled in the lives of Christians that he literally poured out his energy at conferences and conventions, until his body began to complain of the pace set by his spirit. To help him relax, friends financed a period of 'rest-cure treatment' at a Nursing Home in England. He described it in a letter: 'A posh place this, every comfort imaginable! But as for food, I might as well be a donkey—carrots for breakfast, carrots for dinner and carrots for supper!'

Rest-cure and carrots were not enough. The strain of tense services and lengthy sermons caught up with him in Torquay. A spasm of sickness ended his sermon, and he was taken to a friend's home in Plymouth, but insisted on returning to Edinburgh immediately by train. He slept for a few hours on the journey, but woke up feeling dizzy, and each effort to rise brought on sickness. In the darkness he groped for the bell-cord, and the attendant arrived to find him lying in a pool of blood. A doctor on the train alerted the Infirmary in Edinburgh and arranged a blood-transfusion at the station before rushing him to hospital—just in time.

Engagements were cancelled for several months and a six-months' preaching tour of South Africa was also in the balance, but while on holiday in Merligen, Switzerland, with Mrs. Campbell, as the guests of a friend who had been helped through his ministry, he was examined by two specialists from Zurich and given the green light to go, with a caution against preaching more than four times each week.

On 13th December, 1956, he and Mrs. Campbell sailed on the *Capetown Castle*. The boat trip refreshed them and gave Duncan time to study and prepare. He also had the opportunity of conducting a gospel service, but was saddened to see so much drunkenness on board.

Table Mountain was shrouded in thick fog when they docked at Cape Town, but a warm welcome from the Pilgrims of the Africa Evangelistic Band, a sister Mission of the Faith Mission, compensated for that.

The hot climate bothered him, a difficulty he had encountered in Algiers the previous year, but under the anointing of the Holy Spirit he refused to be curtailed in his preaching. An address described as 'a powerful utterance', at the close of a full day and a tiring week, occupied eighty minutes and was followed with close attention, despite the hot atmosphere of a packed hall. His strong Scottish accent and Gaelic pronunciation placed him under a disadvantage with South Africans, but they clung to every word and were deeply moved by the Spirit. The minister of a large Dutch Reformed Church came to his room one night, knelt at the bedside and poured out his heart in confession, asking God to fill him with the Holy Spirit. Other Christian workers were lifted to a new level of fellowship with God.

At a Convention in Cape Town, Duncan, knowing there were some Highlanders in the service, spoke a few words in Gaelic, quoting a Gaelic hymn written by one of the Pilgrims. A man from Lewis accepted Christ that night, testifying to his employer the following day; he in turn became anxious about his soul and went to his minister who pointed him to the Saviour.

Many invitations from churches throughout South Africa were turned down in order to keep within the limits imposed by the doctors, and his programme was further restricted by another mild haemorrhage in Pretoria. A disappointed pastor insisted that the devil had got into his stomach and must be prayed out!

He was greatly refreshed at 'Glenbervie', the home of Captain and Mrs. Dobbie, and with sufficient rest was able to continue his tour; the Captain's parrot encouraged him by repeating: 'Don't worry, try praising!' The fig tree at the bottom of the garden was an added benefit. In the visitors book he wrote: 'Figs, Faith and Fellowship! Happy memories of Glenbervie!'

A special thrill in Pretoria was to hear a pipe band playing *The Green Hills of Tyrol*, but then he writes: 'My sense of rightness was shocked the other day when motoring through a native location to see an old warrior dressed in a kilt of the 42nd Highlanders'—a tartan similar to that of the Campbells of Argyll!

Although dogged by ill-health, his visit to South Africa was greatly blessed, particularly to University students and Christian workers. God used him to kindle new faith and hunger for revival in hearts. The General Superintendent of the A.E.B. remarked: 'We have had more attractive speakers with more spectacular results, but we have never had a more arresting prophet of the Lord than the Rev. Duncan Campbell; the results will be measured more by quality than quantity'—which aptly describes his entire ministry over this period.

On 26th April, he embarked on the *Winchester Castle*—Mrs. Campbell having returned two months earlier—and arrived in Scotland on 11th May to prepare for a new responsibility, to which he had been appointed before his African tour.

CHAPTER NINETEEN

Teaching Others Also

WHEN Mr. Campbell was a student in the Training Home no one could have envisaged that one day he would return to become Principal of the Faith Mission Training Home and Bible College. Without degrees or outstanding intellectual abilities to commend him for the position he had, in the intervening years, been educated in the school of God and graduated with honour in pursuit of God's highest.

His itinerant ministry had included numerous visits to Bible Colleges where his message had profoundly influenced the lives of students. Several missionary societies recognising the value of his experience had already asked him to serve on their councils in an advisory capacity.

The Council of the Mission also saw the wisdom of harnessing the inspiration of Mr. Campbell's witness to influence successive generations of students in the College and invited him to take charge of this 'hub of the Mission'. In April, 1958, he occupied the Principal's study at 18 Ravelston Park.

On mission-fields at home and abroad are scores of young men and women who thank God for spiritual impetus and guidance received from him. He understood the problems of students and shared with them the wealth of his own experiences.

With the help of the visiting lecturers the college curriculum was broadened to accommodate the demand for higher academic standards by missionary societies but he kept the priorities right. Education, programmes, new techniques and methods he took little account of in the work of evangelism, and 'gimmicks' were right out. Not that he despised education or change of methods but these were no substitute for the power of the Holy Spirit.

At a meeting of Bible College principals at the Keswick Convention a veteran missionary said something which reflected his views: 'Our Bible Colleges today are sending out to the mission-field young men and women, well educated, cultured and polished, but destitute of purpose, purity and power!' Mr. Campbell put the emphasis in the proper place.

'Young people get to know God!' he would say, underlining the inadequacy of human resources in Christian service, and how completely sufficient is the power of the Holy Spirit in every situation. His lectures on the Acts of the Apostles demonstrated the sovereignty of the Spirit in evangelism, and no one was better equipped to illustrate from experience the supernatural work of God portrayed here.

He gauged the worth of Christian activity by the measure in which it brought awareness of God and taught his students to do the same. Their business was not to impress people with their own personalities, but to introduce them to God; the vital factor is the atmosphere produced by the presence of God with us, which will penetrate where words fail. This was true in his own life to which students and staff bear testimony. Years before coming to the College as Principal he called one day with

his predecessor and the brief visit left an indelible
impression on the College secretary. She writes: 'They
were praying together and although there is some distance
between the office and study the Presence seemed to fill
the whole atmosphere. I could never forget it. Mr.
Campbell came to the office afterwards and I can still
hear him quietly say: "God's way is via the cross".'

The cross was the secret of God's presence in his life.
For Duncan Campbell it not only represented what
Jesus Christ had done for him; it was a power which
operated daily bringing death to self-interest so that the
life of God had free course through him.

To impress upon the students the conflict involved in
true discipleship he illustrated his talks from wartime
experiences. Christianity was warfare; they were called
to be good soldiers of Jesus Christ and must put on the
whole armour of God, prepared to fight. He recalled
lying in a trench in France with enemy fire sweeping the
lines. Out in front, no man's land was dead men's land—
bodies everywhere! From among the mangled corpses, a
cry floated over to where he lay. A burly Highlander at
his side gave a shout: 'That's Jock o'Blairgowrie! I'll get
him or die in the attempt!' Before anyone could check
him he leapt up and under heavy fire raced to where his
wounded comrade lay and brought him back from
among the dead.

'That's the spirit, young folk, that's the spirit!' the
Principal would say, as he urged students into the battle
for souls. It saddened him when any failed to respond
to the discipline of training which spiritual warfare
required.

His relationship with the students was like that of a
father to his children; they loved him and when con-
flicting points of view, which are inevitable in an inter-

denominational Bible College, arose, Mr. Campbell
respected the convictions of those who differed from him,
endeavouring 'to keep the unity of the spirit in the bond
of peace', not by diplomacy, but by challenging each one
to higher issues of obedience and faith. A new student,
who had never heard of John Calvin or Jacobus Arminius,
went to his study to enquire what this age-old controversy was about. Instead of a long, tedious theological
lecture that would have wearied the untutored mind, he
briefly outlined both viewpoints without trying to
influence the boy either way, then simply exhorted him
to keep close to God, walk in His light and everything
would eventually come clear: 'If any man will do His will
he shall know of the doctrine' (John 7:17).

Friday forenoons in the College were given to prayer
and waiting upon God. These times were the spiritual
highlights of each term. What burning messages he gave!
'We sat trembling as he opened up the Word of God. It
seemed as though God had revealed to him all our inner
attitudes,' said one student. 'But oh, the joy as he lifted us
to new heights of God-realisation! There was something
sacred about the way he used God's name and often the
atmosphere of heaven filled the room when, with rever-
ence and tenderness, he simply said, "Jesus." We felt we
were standing on holy ground.'

It was during one of these prayer-sessions on 4th
March, 1960, that God visited the College in a special
way and did in seconds what others had been trying to do
for months. A deep sense of God filled the place when the
Principal spoke from Habbakuk 2:1: 'I will stand upon
my watch, and set me upon the tower, and will watch to
see what he will say unto me, and what I shall answer
when I am reproved.'

Then as a student began to pray for revival in his own

life the power of God fell upon the group. Some wept silently; others cried out for cleansing. One girl said: 'I never knew what the fear of God was until then; it seemed that if I lifted my head I would look upon God. I never knew what sin was until then; outside the grace of God I felt fit for hell.'

Someone started to sing, 'Jesus keep me near the cross.' Tears of joy flowed as Calvary's healing stream became real. Wave after wave of the Spirit's power brought inner release, equipping many for more effective service. Then heavenly music was heard which seemed to fill the room above where they were kneeling; it was indescribably beautiful and harmonious, such as no orchestra could symphonise, and called to mind Zephaniah 3:17: 'He will rest in His love, He will joy over thee with singing.' This phenomenon was not new to Duncan; at least twice during the Lewis awakening he had heard celestial melodies; once in the early hours of the morning, walking through a glen, the heavens seemed to be filled with angelic praise until another minister present cried out for joy: 'This is heaven! This is heaven!'

Duncan appreciated these manifestations but did not encourage the students to seek them, realising that the devil could gain an advantage in times of spiritual quickening by deflecting attention from the Lord to the phenomena accompanying His work. He sometimes checked excessive emotions with an amusing story: In the early Twenties two Pilgrims had a successful mission at a place called West Benhar. The converts, bursting with joy arrived at a conference in Peebles, and were so full of 'Amens' and 'Hallelujahs', that Mr. Govan had to stop preaching until they quietened. At tea that evening 'the Chief' asked a quaint little Scotsman who was present, to give thanks. He stroked his beard and began: 'Lord, we thank Ye for the conference this afternoon. We thank Ye for the converts frae West Benhar, and for their enthusiasm. But Lord, it must hae grieved Yer hairt tae see sae much o' the steam blowin' oot thro' the whistle that should hae gang tae the piston!'

In cultivating a spiritual atmosphere in the College, Mr. Campbell was far from being sanctimonious. He was natural in his spiritual life, full of humour, and when preparing sermons and lectures would weary for a good cup of tea—and it had to be strong! He was almost cured of this habit one day, when in a moment of absent-mindedness he put a packet of tea into the pot, instead of the tea-caddy; even he could not drink it!

He was tidy when he remembered to be so, but was sometimes unselfconscious to the point of forgetting his personal appearance. About to enter the dining-room for meals or lectures another member of staff might draw attention to his hair, give it a quick comb which he would accept with good grace, before going in! On a preaching tour he was not so fortunate to have this personal super-vision and once, much to his amusement, the chairman, a Dane, prayed for him in quaint simplicity: 'Lord, bless this Thy shaggy prophet whom Thou hast sent to us from the Hebrides!'

He disliked spring cleaning! 'What a blanock!' he would say when the students invaded his study for the annual clean-up. At least there was no litter problem: all letters and papers were attended to with as little delay as possible, so quickly that the secretary sometimes had to rescue them from the waste-paper basket in case they should be needed for future reference!

His unselfconsciousness was further reflected the first time he heard himself preaching on tape. 'That's not me!' he emphatically announced after listening awhile. He disliked tape recorders, but was too tender-hearted to refuse those who asked permission to record his messages.

In 1965 an attack of Ménière's Disease resulting in loss of balance, threatened to terminate his ministry. Several sudden falls nearly caused serious injury. The matron and secretary tried to dissuade him from going to a series of conferences in East Anglia, but his mind was made up. 'I will be all right if I have someone with me and something to lean on when I'm preaching.'

The Mission director took him by car, and assisted him to the pulpit for the opening service. The following morning the rector from a nearby church called at the home where Duncan was staying, and ignoring his apology for being unable to rise, quietly asked: 'Mr. Campbell, would you like to be healed?'

'If that's the Lord's will, I certainly would,' replied Duncan, cautiously.

Placing his hand on the sick men's shoulder the minister prayed simply and earnestly: 'Dear Jesus, please heal Mr. Campbell, so that he can continue with his ministry.'

Like an electric shock, the power of God went through his body; he was healed! Not only was his body healed; his mental powers were so quickened that in the following weeks he prepared more new sermons than he had done in the previous few years. His secretary had to work overtime to keep up with him!

Later, writing to the minister who had prayed for him, Duncan records: 'I have had no recurrence at all of the disease since you prayed for me. There can be no doubt but that God miraculously touched me. I am so grateful to Him, and to you for your earnest prayer.'

Next to God, preaching was Duncan's chief desire. When bogged down with administration problems it refreshed him to go off on a preaching trip. Sometimes he was criticised for being away too often from the College, but it is unlikely that he could have continued with his responsibilities there had it not been for the reinvigorating effect that preaching had upon him. A student who took him to Paisley saw his youth renewed in the pulpit in much the same way as James Melville described John Knox preaching at St. Andrews: 'He was lifted up to the pulpit, where he behoved to lean at his first entry. But, ere he had done with his sermon, he was so active and vigorous, that he was like to ding that pulpit in blads (break it in pieces!) and flee out of it.' There was no discrimination in his bookings; he was as willing to speak to half-a-dozen nurses at the Christian Fellowship in the infirmary, as to address a large convention.

Due to retire in 1963 he agreed to remain at the College for a further three years until a successor was appointed, but during these years he strained at the leash, longing to be free to devote himself entirely to convention and conference ministry. On this battleground God blessed him most, and the message of holiness and revival he was given to proclaim burned like a fire within, seeking an outlet before his course would finish.

CHAPTER TWENTY

Prophet at Large

RELEASED from College duties a rugged, uncompromising prophet invaded the Christian scene, which in the early sixties had become shallow and mediocre, and penetrated with materialism. Content to imitate the methods and organisations of the world in an effort to retain adherents, many religious bodies were unconcerned that 'the stream of vital Christianity was running low', as Duncan put it.

The burden of his preaching was a plea for reality—the reality of God coming within the bounds of human personality through an indwelling Christ. He often said that the most solemn thing about any man is the unconscious influence of his personality, which daily leads others to God, or away from God. 'What the world needs to see is the wonder and beauty of God-possessed personalities; men and women with the life of God pulsating within, who practise the presence of God and consequently make it easy for others to believe in God.' Witness the testimony of a young man, now a schoolteacher, to this moral power operating in a life:

To him religion was a rather boring business without any attraction. He lived for the world of sport until one day, gazing through a window, just day-dreaming, he saw a man with hands behind his back, going for a stroll. He did not know him then, had never spoken to him or seen him before. The man was moving away from him, but as the young fellow watched there arose within him an overwhelming conviction: 'There, that is what you have been looking for all your life. I'd give anything to have what that man has!'

The powerful impression suddenly fastened upon him he describes more fully:

This man had a beauty for me that I craved, and it had nothing to do with his face or his human characteristics—I was looking at his back. Was it possible that God could so merge with a man that for me Christ and Duncan Campbell were indistinguishable? That was how it seemed, and yet the craving started that day was not for this strange man, but for God in Christ. I never saw God until that day, and in the days that followed the vision lingered and haunted me till I was 'found'. I heard other men preach, earnest and sincere, and with honest endeavour; they affected my thoughts and ideas, but the reality I discovered that day was embodied in a personality. The man Campbell made me, without knowing it, to face truth and reality personified. And this left me facing—Christ!

An anonymous poet wrote of a similiar experience:

> Not merely in the words you say,
>   Not only in your deeds confessed,
> But in the most unconscious way,
>   Is Christ expressed.

For me, 'twas not the truth you taught,
  To you so clear, to me still dim,
But when you came to me you brought,
  A sense of Him.

Killadeas Camp Convention in Northern Ireland was
a favourite resort of Mr. Campbell's. It was here that
the above incident occurred. He loved the unhurried,
rough and ready atmosphere, steeped in prayer, and from
a little bush-shaded shack (known as 'Duncan's Castle'),
on the hillock overlooking the camp grounds, he could
gaze out across the waters of Lough Erne. It reminded
him of his own Highlands. How he laughed when he first
occupied this eight-by-five feet dwelling, originally built
as a hen-house, when a hefty Irishman came in, ham-
mered a six-inch nail into the wall and announced:
'Your wardrobe, Mr. Campbell!'

One who met with God at the camp writes: 'What
sacred memories linger of those visits; days of heaven on
earth, when God came down in awful majesty and the
stones and trees around seemed alive with His Presence.'
Duncan, thrilled with the atmosphere, sometimes booked
himself into his 'castle' for the following year before the
conveners had time to invite him again!

The simplicity of this down-to-earth environment
appealed to him; he could make himself at home in any
society, and occasionally enjoyed being entertained in
more wealthy surroundings, but had little desire for
luxurious living. Eating salted herring and new potatoes
in a humble Highland croft was more like prophet's
fare, and nearer the spirit of his Master who had no-
where to lay His head.

Evangelical witness in Ireland would be poorer today
but for the frequent trips that Duncan Campbell made

across the Irish Sea. He took a keen interest in Christian work there, and through his preaching many revival prayer-groups sprang up through the country. At a memorable Convention in Lisburn in 1964 he declared: 'Ireland will have riots and revival!' The first part of this prophecy has been grimly fulfilled, and a foretaste of the latter was received on the final day of the Convention.

After breakfast, Duncan retired to his room to wait upon God. His host, the Convention chairman, was sitting alone in the dining-room when suddenly he became aware of 'the brightness of the Presence of the Lord'. So awe-inspiring did it become that he felt unworthy to be in the room and went out to the garden. There, plants and flowers were resplendent with the same brightness; he was melted to tears and returned to the house, wondering. Then Duncan, his face aglow, appeared. 'God has given me a vision concerning revival for Ireland,' he said, and described how God would visit the island through small bands of praying people in the country districts.

This strange, enveloping sense of God's Presence remained throughout the day. That evening Duncan preached his final address and pronounced the bene-diction when, as one present said: 'God took over the service.' The organist attempted to play a voluntary but her hands were powerless to reach the keyboard; the congregation was gripped by an awe-full stillness so that no one moved for over half-an-hour. Then some began to pray and weep. God worked deeply in hearts, and during the stillness at least four people heard indescrib-able sounds from heaven, inaudible to others.

Travelling home from one of these services, a farmer uttered one of the highest tributes that could be paid to a preacher. Turning to his companions he said: 'You never hear Campbell preach without going home to pray.'

South Wales was another centre which at a crucial time in its spiritual history felt the impact of God through Duncan Campbell's ministry. Following the revival of 1904-5 unhealthy divisions existed between the witness of the churches and independent mission-halls. Duncan's experience of both church and mission-work helped him to bridge the gap. When he first visited Wales in the late fifties the Christians were concentrating on denominational issues. He stepped in and asked: 'Is God real?' They got a jolt! God had almost been displaced in the midst of His work! During successive visits barriers melted in the lives of those willing to face the challenge of his message, and one far-reaching result was the renewed prayer-life of many Christians.

The outstanding occasion of his ministry in the Principality was in Aberdare. Much prayer had gone up for a short series of meetings in this little town and after the second service a prayer-meeting was held which continued until three o'clock the following morning. Expectancy ran high and several Christians took time off from their employment to pray throughout the following day. The minister who convened the services remarked: 'I believe something is going to happen in the meeting tonight!'

An eye-witness says:

When Mr. Campbell had spoken for an hour six young men seated together saw 'the glory of God' come down upon him. A great fear came upon them and they fell to the floor weeping. Fear also gripped the congregation; many were overwhelmed by a sense of sin and scenes of repentance and restoration followed as one

and another made things right between themselves
and God . . .
Duncan Campbell taught us many things, but above
all we learned that it is God, not man, we need today.

The message he proclaimed was above the usual
controversial issues among evangelicals. Consequently he
preached in almost every Protestant denomination in the
British Isles. Invited to speak at a large congress of the
Apostolic Church in Wales, he felt it a duty to clarify his
position before accepting and mentioned that he was 'a
hard-boiled Presbyterian', who could not share the view
that speaking in tongues was the evidence of being
baptised in the Holy Spirit. The invitation was renewed,
assuring him that his views were well-known 'but the
message you are proclaiming is the message the church
needs today.'

In Europe and across the Atlantic, reports of the
Hebridean awakening and three small volumes of
sermons by Mr. Campbell, whetted the appetites of
Christians to hear him. Faith Mission work had reached
the shores of France and Canada, and was refreshed by
visits from this beloved leader from the homeland.

Canada was of particular interest to Mr. Campbell.
He told audiences of his debt to the Canadian trooper
who had saved his life in France, and was actually
introduced to a veteran of the Canadian regiment who
fought in the battle. He hoped then to meet his bene-
factor, but never did. Apart from this personal interest,
God had placed upon him a prayer-burden for revival in
the vast Dominion; a burden shared by small bands of
intercessors, who were concerned that Canada had never
known widespread revival. The burden was transmitted
to many more as he thundered out a rebuke of the

careless, shallow ways of modern evangelism. A minister, requesting his prayers, wrote that aspirations, dimmed by the stress of human circumstances, were restored to see the possibilities of revival.

Another writes: 'At that time when so many settled down into thinking that deep, lasting revival would no longer be experienced Mr. Campbell proved otherwise, and in this his voice was the voice of God.'

In June 1969 he preached in a small Baptist church in Saskatoon, Saskatchewan. The pastor longed for a genuine movement of the Spirit, and had been guided for three years to pray that God would send Duncan Campbell to his church. During this campaign attendance was small, but desire for God was intensified. The spirit of expectancy deepened so that a minister who attended said: 'I know that shortly we shall see revival!' One night the preacher prophesied that Canada would see revival and that it would begin in that very church.

Two years later, Saskatoon suddenly hit the headlines—'*Is Canada seeing Revival?*' '*Saskatoon: Vortex of Revival*' '*Renewed Morality Found in Wake of Revival*'— so ran the press reports. What began as a typical evangelistic campaign mushroomed into a spiritual awakening. The church was packed, and the venue moved three times until a large auditorium was necessary to accommodate the people. The Holy Spirit moved quietly and powerfully: church leaders and Christian workers confessed sin and were reconciled to each other; businessmen in the city were surprised when people called to pay for stolen goods; broken homes were restored, alcoholics and drug addicts delivered, and countless numbers freed from the bondage of self and satanic oppression to witness effectively for Christ. Reports indicated similar happenings in other centres throughout Western Canada.

A short time before news of this awakening began to reach the British Isles, Duncan Campbell, at his home in Edinburgh, was especially moved one day to spend two hours in prayer for Canada and was assured that God was moving there. Perhaps that was the very day God broke through in Saskatoon! Certainly, he was 'in touch' with the purposes of God in the world.

Across the border in the United States he was welcomed back where he had never been before! Some popularity-seeking, religious showman had apparently impersonated him years before he first crossed the Atlantic! But when he appeared in reality, his preaching was blessed with the same power as in Canada and elsewhere.

At a Bible Conference in Rockford, Illinois, Duncan met a young couple, Loren Cunningham and his wife, who were praying about opening a School of Evangelism in Europe. The idea was to establish a centre where young people could be taught by visiting lecturers on various aspects of evangelism, and field-trips organised through European and Middle Eastern countries to prepare them for work amongst people of differing cultures and religious backgrounds.

Through contact with Duncan this vision was confirmed as God's plan, and a spacious hotel building over-looking the Savoy Alps, situated on the edge of Switzerland's largest pine forest, near Lausanne, was purchased. Duncan, always prayerfully concerned with other people's interests in the work of God, followed each step in the development of the school, and among staff and students became one of its best-loved lecturers; his subject of course—*Evangelism and Revival*.

He had the distinction of being the oldest teacher to visit the school, and by comparison with the students,

who were mostly products of modern society, appeared
at first as a reserved Scottish Highlander. Yet there
was no generation gap; his love and sympathy and
the spiritual impact of his personality bridged all
cultural, social and mental divisions—he didn't turn
them off!

Successive sessions of students came under the spell
of the Highland prophet in Switzerland, and also in
Greece, where he ministered to a group in the beautiful
fishing-village of Porto-Rafti on the Aegean Sea. The
outstanding feature of his ministry was the unique way
in which he reproduced himself in the lives of these young
people. Several young, married couples who came under
his influence in Greece later became leaders of spiritual
advance in Europe.

Here is a student's personal reminiscences of one of
his sermons:

Prior to Mr. Campbell's coming we thought we had
arrived! Then conviction came, *real conviction*. Small
things we thought were harmless became sins in our
sight. For example, we used to take cookies from the
kitchen—we called it 'snitching', but God called it
stealing. It was shattering to be seen as a thief! Such
incidents were confessed and put right and God
consolidated His work in us.

What was invested in their lives, lives on. With faith
strengthened and encouraged to believe God for similar
manifestations of His power they spread across the
world to serve Him. One witnessed an outpouring of
the Spirit in a small town in Ioha, U.S.A. when God came
down in a unique way and over 200 young people sought
Christ. He said: 'It showed me that what Duncan

Campbell said was true. God can move in a sovereign way without any publicity stunts or gimmicks.'

But with the 'waste of seas' and foreign hills between, the heart was still Highland. In dreams he beheld the Hebrides, and always longed to return to the scene of former conflicts and triumphs. World-wide travels were punctuated with pilgrimages to his 'promised land' and any fresh spark of the Spirit's power was meat and drink to his soul. A convert of the revival, now ordained, invited him to his church in Lemreway to preach at a communion season and here Duncan felt the old fire kindling in the parish. At the Thanksgiving Service before returning to Edinburgh, he predicted that the congregation was on the verge of revival, and during the next few weeks the genial power of the Spirit moved in the district bringing many to Christ.

In the summer of 1971 he returned to Stornoway for the Convention. Usually enthusiastic, and full of suggestions for future campaigns and conventions, he was noticeably quiet and withdrawn. Someone spoke to him about future plans which he discussed thoughtfully, but added: 'This may be my last Stornoway Convention.' Just a passing comment—but it stuck.

CHAPTER TWENTY-ONE

'So Fight I'

Be strong!
It matters not how deep entrenched the wrong;
How hard the battle goes, the day how long;
Faint not, fight on! Tomorrow comes the song.

Maltbie Davenport Babcock.

WITH heather and moss-covered stones for cushions, and sheep grazing around, an old weather-beaten shepherd and a young evangelist sat on the hillside talking together about God.

Observing the tired, tense attitude of the younger man the shepherd cautioned: 'Ye'll be needin' tae look after yersel, an' be takin' things easier, ah'm seein'.'

'Take things easier!' snorted the other, surprised and indignant. 'Take things easier, and souls perishing! I'd rather burn out than rust out!'

'Aye, aye, son,' nodded the wise old hill-dweller, 'But ye ken its better tae mak' it last oot!'

Duncan liked to recall this advice he received as a young man, and after half-a-century of 'burning out' he was still 'lastin' oot'. True, ill-health had dogged his footsteps; lesser men would have thrown in the sponge long ago and called it a day, but he fought bravely on against physical limitations, as well as spiritual opposition.

Like Oswald Chambers, he believed that antagonism is the basis of life in the physical realm as well as in the moral and spiritual. He maintained an inner fighting vitality which offset bodily ailments, and repeatedly trusted God to quicken his body by the Holy Spirit, when normal rest was insufficient to restore his strength.

Through many brushes with death he reaffirmed what Thomas Boston wrote years before that 'man is immortal till his work is done'. Not until God refused to have him any longer out of His nearer Presence would the long fight for survival in the body be over.

God always provides for those who consistently try to serve Him, and in a neat little bungalow in Edinburgh gifted by a friend, he could have enjoyed a fireside-chair retirement. But the word 'retirement' was not in his vocabulary; the sound of battle was in his soul, and, like Whitefield, he would fain die, sword in hand.

While the inner man was renewed constantly, the outer frame which had endured the exertions of childhood, battlefield and pulpit was beginning to wear. It was obvious to those intimately acquainted with him that the fire of earlier years had abated; the voice was weaker, the manner less forceful, though the words still had the same penetrating weight—the same man was behind them. Now and then he would burst forth in a blaze of vitality, straining once more for revival days.

The vision of greater revivals mastered any tyranny of success in his thinking, and stripped him of satisfaction with past victories. He was eager to pursue new spiritual achievements. A Gaelic proverb—'The man who will not look ahead of him will look behind'—reminded him of the danger of living in the past.

On that memorable night when the revival broke out in Barvas church an elder, surveying the scene, turned to Duncan and said: 'Mr. Campbell, you have lived to see this day; now you will live in the memory of it.'

Recounting the incident to his students some years later he cried: 'Live in the memory of it! Never! We must live for greater things! No victory is secure except by greater victories!' Not for him the image of the old soldier in the drawing-room, or on the street-corner, inflating his ego with the memory of battles fought long ago while there are still enemies on the field to conquer. The past must be inspiration for the future. In the past is the seed of hope for future victory. God has done it before; God can do it again! Revival he had seen; revival he *must* see. If not, with his own eyes, then he must labour that others may witness it. He dreamed of the day when all Scotland would be revived and imbued again with the spirit of the covenanters and reformers to stand for 'the crown rights of the Redeemer'.

Fighting back from a mild cerebral haemorrhage in the autumn of 1971 he planned a full programme for the coming year. In March he returned to Lausanne to the School of Evangelism, staying a few days with his daughter, Sheena, en route. Twice each day he spoke to the students on various aspects of Christian experience and between lectures, sitting in a swing chair on the lawn with cow-bells tinkling in the meadow nearby and the fragrance of pine-trees in the air, they gathered spontaneously around, as he shared personal reminiscences of God's hand upon his life.

Challenge and inspiration came to many during those weeks. A German fellow in particular, a former hippy 'guru', converted to Christianity in Morocco six months before, was introduced to a new realm of spiritual revolution. The 'truth' of Christianity and the satisfying answers it provided to his questions thrilled him; his keen intellect had absorbed the lectures of successive teachers at the school, then:

> Duncan Campbell came, and I saw God was not a subject for the intellect only. There was a personal dimension missing in my life which this man radiated. He personified the teachings of all the other teachers who came to the school. It was not so much what he said that gripped me but the man behind the words— his Christlikeness. Jesus was real to him.

On he battled. New territory in lives was being taken from the enemy and dedicated to his King and he rejoiced. Then on Thursday morning after a special time of blessing around God's Word the Director in charge noticed his tired condition and suggested that he rest for the remainder of the day, and someone else could speak in the evening. For two days a recurring pain, which he regarded as indigestion, had bothered him, but he was determined to soldier on for the final lecture of the series. He replied: 'God has given me a message for the meeting this evening. I must deliver it. Please do not stand in God's way.'

The text for the service was typical of his life: 'So fight I, not as one that beateth the air.' Christian experience, he reminded them, is more than the sound of happy laughter mingled with the singing of birds; it is a battle. There are enemies without, and enemies in the garrison of the soul to contend with, hence real Christianity will never be in vogue. 'The New Testament reveals Jesus as a realist. He will never be popular; His followers need never expect to be. He will have men follow Him knowing the cost . . .

it means a fight!' Calling each student to stand with faith and courage beneath the banner of the cross of Christ, his last words were: 'Keep on fighting, but see that you are fighting in the love of Jesus!'

Moved by this message the young folk gathered afterwards for a prayer-meeting and asked him to join them. He did so for a while, but feeling exhausted retired to bed.

At 2 a.m. the attack came. He was removed to the Cantonal Hospital, and attached to a heart monitor with a recording graph and warning bell. Mrs. Campbell and Sheena came to his side and for four days he progressed satisfactorily, remaining cheerful and courteous and concerned about all those who came to see him.

Then the summons came—swift and sparing. After tests on the evening of Tuesday, 28th March, the graph took a sudden dive, the bell rang and the battle was over.

Died with the sound of battle round him rolled,
And rumour of battle in all nations' hearts;
Dying, saw his life a thing
Of large beginnings; and for young
Hands yet untrained the harvesting,
Amid the iniquitous years if harvest sprung.
                                         Francis Thompson

Harvest has sprung! Harvest will spring!

Looking across the bay from the old homestead in which Duncan Campbell was born, the granite stone of Ardchattan Church glints in the sunlight. A mantle of furze and bracken clothes the hillside behind.

There, where he desired to lie, amidst the beauty and grandeur of the Highlands he loved, and where the sound of battle no longer disturbs, his earthly remains await the sound of the trumpet on the resurrection morning.

THE FAITH MISSION

was instituted by the late J. G. Govan in 1886 for the Evangelising of the Country Districts of Great Britain and Ireland. For further information write to:

The Faith Mission,
Govan House,
38 Coates Gardens,
Edinburgh EH12 5LD.